AMAZING STORIES

CRIME BOSS KILLINGS

AMAZING STORIES

CRIME BOSS KILLINGS
The Castellammarese War

GANGSTER
by Art Montague

PUBLISHED BY ALTITUDE PUBLISHING LTD.
1500 Railway Avenue, Canmore, Alberta T1W 1P6
www.altitudepublishing.com
1-800-957-6888

Copyright 2005 © Art Montague
All rights reserved
First published 2005

Extreme care has been taken to ensure that all information presented in this book is accurate and up to date. Neither the author nor the publisher can be held responsible for any errors.

Publisher	Stephen Hutchings
Associate Publisher	Kara Turner
Series Editor	Jill Foran
Editor	Lori Burwash
Digital Photo Colouring	Bryan Pezzi

We acknowledge the financial support of the Government of Canada through the Book Publishing Industry Development Program (BPIDP) for our publishing activities.

Altitude GreenTree Program
Altitude Publishing will plant twice as many trees as were used in the manufacturing of this product.

Cataloging in Publication Data

Montague, Art
 Crime boss killings / Art Montague.

(Amazing stories)
ISBN 1-55265-101-0

 1. Black Hand (United States)--History. 2. Mafia--New York (State)--New York--
History--20th century. I. Title. II. Series: Amazing stories (Canmore, Alta.)

HV6446.M65 2005   364.1'06'09747109043
C2005-902432-1

An application for the trademark for Amazing Stories™
has been made and the registered trademark is pending.

Printed and bound in Canada by Friesens
2 4 6 8 9 7 5 3 1

The history of organized crime in New York City has long been glamorized through books, magazines, film, and television. Inevitably, anyone researching this history will be presented with many different "true accounts" of underworld events. In regards to each title in the Amazing Stories series, Altitude Publishing has left it up to the author to choose which version of events he or she wishes to convey.

Contents

Prologue 11

Chapter 1 Right Place, Right Time 13

Chapter 2 The Party Crasher 30

Chapter 3 Neutrality, New York City Style 42

Chapter 4 The Luck of Lucky Luciano 57

Chapter 5 Pick Your Poison 67

Chapter 6 Peacetime Plotting 79

Chapter 7 Checkmate 95

Chapter 8 Crime Pays 104

Epilogue 112

Prologue

April 15, 1931. Though the air was still cool and crisp, the warm spring breezes drew New Yorkers out onto the streets. At lunchtime, office workers in Manhattan found reasons to get out of their buildings, eating their sandwiches as they strolled. The heart of the city was picking up its beat.

Out at Coney Island, things weren't quite as active so early in the season. However, one neighborhood business was busy on this day, the Nuova Villa Tammaro, an upscale Italian eatery. Its owner, Gerardo Scarpato, had worked all morning preparing a very special meal for some very special people — people known throughout much of New York as men with very big appetites, in more ways than one.

By 3:30 that afternoon only two members of the lunch party remained in the restaurant, lingering over espressos and a game of cards at a back table. Scarpato had cleared the table and piled the dishes for the dish washer, who would come on duty in about an hour. With part of the sunny afternoon still available and his customers contentedly occupied, he decided to go for a brief walk.

Scarpato wasn't gone long, perhaps only 15 minutes. As he began sauntering back to check on his customers, police cars, sirens blaring, sped past him. He saw the cars brake in front of his restaurant and police, guns drawn, rush through his door. He ran for the restaurant, where two uniformed patrolmen not only barred entry but jammed him against a wall. One roughly frisked him, while his partner pressed a gun against the back of his head.

Inside the restaurant, the police faced carnage. Paneling on the back wall had been shredded by bullets. On the floor, clutching part of a bloodstained tablecloth, was a dead man. Several bullets had struck his head, but police still recognized him, and they were not surprised.

Sitting at a table, calmly smoking a cigarette, was a slim, well-dressed young man. He had called the police, but he'd seen nothing. Nor, of course, had Scarpato. This was the way things happened during the Castellammarese War.

Chapter 1
Right Place, Right Time

At the turn of the 20th century, New York City's numerous Unione Siciliane and Mafia gangs tended not to litter the streets with bodies of competitors or enemies. Generally, they would bury them in out-of-the-way places or cremate them in the coal and wood furnaces that heated most buildings. Occasionally, they made exceptions. Informants from within their own ranks were one of these. For them was reserved a more public fate that the newspapers dubbed "barrel murders" after the corpse of Benedetto Madonia was found partly stuffed in a barrel of sawdust in 1903. He had been stabbed repeatedly, his throat cut from ear to ear. The Mob's message was clear: "Don't rat!" The so-called men of honor apparently took themselves and their rules very seriously.

Crime Boss Killings

During the first two decades of the new century, being a "man of honor" didn't count for much outside New York's Italian and Sicilian neighborhoods. Within those neighborhoods, rivalries between the Sicilian and Italian gangs often reached a flashpoint. For most, the Old World villages or provinces from which they came were far more important than the country. The concept of country bespoke conquerors — 2000 years of them for Sicilians.

Italians had also suffered their share of conquerors, as well as homegrown dictators. In the villages and provinces of both lands, self-defense groups formed. In mainland Italy, they became known as Camorra or Mafia. In Sicily, they were known as the Unione Siciliane or Black Hand. At first, these groups were regarded by the peasants as Robin Hoods, but as their power grew, they ceased to be protectors and became exploiters. Rich and poor alike were their victims. In their respective environs, the individual criminal factions also preyed upon one another.

The Tyrrhenian Sea separated Sicily and Italy, somewhat reducing conflict between the Unione Siciliane and Mafia. But in New York City and other major US cities, there was no sea of separation, only neighborhood boundaries defined by the immigrant populations and, often, the immigrants' ties to their homeland. Enemies for centuries, the Italian Mafia and Sicilian Unione were destined to import their conflict to America.

Indeed, ties to the Old Country went beyond nostalgia

Right Place, Right Time

or generations'-old feuds. The ties of New York City immigrants went deep into the Unione in Sicily and the Mafia in mainland Italy, both of which, during this period, were immensely powerful. For example, one of their most lucrative rackets at the turn of the century was counterfeiting, a practice so prevalent it had reached the potential to destabilize national economies.

The source of much of the counterfeit American currency passed in the United States was Sicily. In New York City, the local Unione Siciliane gangsters coerced shopkeepers — often first-generation Italians or Sicilians — into putting the counterfeit into circulation. This was relatively easy to achieve since most shopkeepers were already paying protection to the gangsters, were indebted to their loan sharks, or were doing some bookmaking for the local gang.

New York's Mafia and Unione Siciliane factions were probably making a good living, but none had hit the big time at the turn of the 20th century. Big time were the Irish gangs, who had a grip on Tammany Hall (the political power of the day) and who held sway on the docks — protection, pilferage, warehouse raids, and also the usual small-time gambling and extortion. The Irish gangs were the worms in the Big Apple.

Top to bottom, Denny Meehan was the Irish boss on the Brooklyn docks. At the top, the shipping companies paid protection. At the bottom, Meehan's "white hands" took a fee from every longshoreman's wages by controlling the daily shape-up — the determination of who worked and who didn't.

Crime Boss Killings

Until as late as 1919, Meehan held sway over the docks. Not only that, he had significantly embarrassed an Old Country mobster boss, Giuseppe "Battista" Balsamo. Battista had come over from Sicily in 1895 with blue-chip credentials. He was able to make some early moves to establish himself in the Red Hook district, a part of the Brooklyn docks complex. It didn't last. Meehan's gang moved in and chipped out some substantial pieces of Battista's territory.

Frank Yale, née Francesco Uale, another key Unione Siciliane Brooklyn boss, had respect for tradition. As a matter of that respect, he tried to shore up Battista, who was in his 40s by then — for wiseguys, practically pensionable. Strategically, shoring up Battista would help Yale gain more respect and influence among his peers, weaken Meehan's organization by spreading his forces thinner, and penetrate Meehan's hold on territory that Yale considered his exclusive preserve. Nor was it lost on Yale that inevitably he could become Battista's heir, extending his own power onto the Red Hook docks. Yale was doing well, but he didn't have the docks, where the real money was. So he went after a Meehan plum, the Gowanus pier protection racket.

Yale served notice on Gowanus Stevedoring that the company would now pay his people for protection. How Meehan's people would react to this was incidental to Yale. Gowanus agreed, but, showing appropriate due diligence, the company informed Meehan of the change in "insurance agents."

Benjamin "Crazy Benny" Pazzo was the designated

Right Place, Right Time

collector of Yale's first payment on the Gowanus deal, a singular honor for Gowanus Stevedoring because Crazy Benny was Yale's premier enforcer, sent out only on the most important of jobs. Snow had fallen the night before, effectively shutting down the pier. Crazy Benny trudged from the car, heading for the Gowanus office. Suddenly, his solitary footprints in the snow were joined by three other sets: those of Meehan himself and his top shooters, Wild Bill Lovett and Pegleg Lonergan. The Irishmen walked Crazy Benny to the end of the pier, shot him dead, and threw him into the river — perhaps the first long walk on a short pier. Yale had started a Brooklyn war.

Within weeks, Meehan was shot dead in his bed. Wild Bill took over Meehan's operations, and the war went public. Yale prevailed upon his good friend Al Capone to send two of his best shooters from Chicago for a special job. The two, John Scalise and Albert Anselmo, arrived by train, then duly shot up Brooklyn's Sagaman Hall, where 36 members of Wild Bill's gang, plus wives and girlfriends, were having a night on the town. Three people were killed and nine others wounded. Shortly after, Wild Bill responded. Four shooters burst into a Yale party at Stauch's Dancehall on Coney Island. This time, five were killed, including one of the Irish shooters, and nine wounded.

By 1920, Yale had firm control of Unione Siciliane affairs in Brooklyn. There were still splinter groups in the neighborhoods, such as Battista's, but these had seen the wisdom of accepting Yale's approach to business — that is, consolidation of Unione territory (made easier by Battista's willingness to retire) and expansion beyond the Sicilian neighborhood enclaves into all of Brooklyn. Yale's organization was now stronger than all the others in Brooklyn put together.

Frank Yale's power was such that he became the de facto national leader of the Unione, more a sop to his ego than a position of authority. For example, while he had good relations with Unione factions in Manhattan, he had no part in their day-to-day criminal affairs. And over in Manhattan, things were just as nasty as in Brooklyn. In Upper Manhattan, the powerful Morello-Terranova Gang was gutted when two of its top leaders were sentenced to long federal prison terms for counterfeiting. At 21 years of age, Ciro Terranova, a Morello relative, assumed a major leadership role.

The Morello-Terranova Gang was a family clan with strong ties to Sicily and the Unione. By the time Ciro took over leadership, the gang was a force in East Harlem, not only working traditional rackets but also involved in the narcotics trade. As Yale was expanding into Mafia territory in Brooklyn, the Morello-Terranova Gang was doing the same in Harlem, which was then a predominantly Italian and Sicilian part of Manhattan. However, whereas Yale tended to use guile to get his way, Morello-Terranova used muscle.

The Mafia in Harlem was not taking this incursion lying down. Soon, disputes were littering the streets with bodies. As early as 1912, five mobsters were killed on a busy street

Right Place, Right Time

corner. In 1915 and 1916, the disputes between the Sicilians and Italians heated up as the Unione pressured Italian shopkeepers to pass counterfeit money and deal narcotics. Key leaders on both sides were slain.

The police carried out perfunctory investigations, but the rule of silence prevailed. In frustration, the police decided the Unione Siciliane and Camorra were simply at it again, with neither side willing to talk, even when a man was caught with a smoking gun. By then, disposal of corpses was being left to the coroner's office. Death had become so routine that neither side felt any need to hide bodies or wait until dark to commit murder.

But in Manhattan's Lower East Side and, indeed, in Upper Manhattan, other criminal forces were "earning their bones" and negotiating fragile alliances motivated by power, greed, and poverty. Many of the ambitious, ruthless young men, some still in their teens, who would later head up New York's crime families and other crime families across the country had begun rising through the ranks. Sometimes they showed up on police blotters.

Brooklyn's Frank Yale was one example. His name first appeared there in 1912, charged with disorderly conduct. In 1913, 16-year-old Vito Genovese arrived in New York City ready, willing, and able to make his mark. In 1917, he was arrested for carrying a gun. Under the tutelage of Lucky Luciano, also a youth at the time, Genovese would eventually rise to head Luciano's "family." Salvatore Sabella, who first killed a man when he was 14 and was then spirited to America by the Unione Siciliane, was already active in Philadelphia, where he would eventually rise to become the city's Unione czar. Sabella's first stop had been New York City, where he learned the ropes in Cola Shiro's family and formed alliances that would last through the 1920s. Another New York expatriate, so to speak, was Al Capone, a boyhood chum of Yale. Capone had to flee to Chicago to escape probable arrest and conviction for a gang-related murder.

In 1915, Francesco Castiglio, later known as Frank Costello, was slapped with a year in jail for carrying a concealed weapon. Less than a year later, young Charlie Luciano got himself a one-year sentence for drug possession and trafficking. His close boyhood friend, Meyer Lansky, was instrumental in getting him an early parole. Lansky's intervention was unique, perhaps the seed for many subsequent years of close criminal cooperation between Luciano's outfit and a loose-knit group some writers and law enforcement officials came to call "the Kosher Nostra."

Besides Meyer Lansky, several other non-Sicilians or non-Italians who would have major roles in the underworld were beginning to emerge. In 1909, an enterprising young man named Arnold Rothstein opened his first gambling parlor. Around the same time, Owney "the Killer" Madden, who led a gang called the Gophers, decisively overcame his chief competition, the Hudson Dusters. He earned tremendous cachet by surviving an assassination attempt in which he was

Right Place, Right Time

shot five times.

All the while, Giuseppe Masseria was ascending toward leadership of Manhattan's Unione. Masseria arrived in New York City in 1903. He was 24 years old when he stepped off the boat at Ellis Island. By then, he was already a seasoned Unione Siciliane enforcer, having learned his craft in his native Palermo. Masseria had been hastened to America because of a law enforcement crackdown in Palermo that had placed him on Sicily's most wanted list. His English was shaky, but that didn't matter — most of his business was conducted from inside New York's Sicilian neighborhoods. Indeed, he lived in the same Lower East Side house throughout his life in America.

The Morello-Terranova family welcomed Masseria with open arms. The man was a Palermo top gun, literally. An old-school Unione member, Masseria played by the rules laid down by the Unione hundreds of years previously, when its members were battling conquerors from the mainland. He executed orders without question. If he embarked on an enterprise of his own, he always cleared it first with his boss and, afterward, always ensured that the boss got a piece of the proceeds. This respect in the form of tribute was completely just and right in Masseria's view because a man of honor always showed respect. He gave it and, later, he demanded it of his own underlings.

Two other qualities made Masseria a standout. First, he was a good earner. When he was sent to make a collection, he always got it — always the full count, never any excuses. His second standout quality — he kept his mouth shut. Joseph Valachi, an infamous government witness, later described this attribute as *omerta*, a cardinal rule of the Unione dictating that members will not give information to outsiders.

How Masseria earned his money was somewhat demonstrated in 1907, when he received a suspended sentence on burglary and extortion convictions. The burglary charge likely arose from Masseria's day job, independent criminal activity apart from work carried out for Unione bosses. The extortion charge was probably related to Masseria's protection rackets. More important, for Masseria to have more or less walked away from such convictions without prison terms suggests "the fix" was in, probably through the influence of Giosue Gallucci.

Gallucci was a smooth wheeler-dealer. He bribed, he cajoled, and he manipulated. He also stood apart from ethnic factionalism — although an Italian, he had no qualms about serving Unione Siciliane interests. He was a key contact for the Morello-Terranova Gang, but he was his own boss, balancing his activities on a tightrope of mediation and influence in sectors the street gangs could not reach. Much of his power derived from his ability to deliver Harlem's Italian and Sicilian vote to Tammany at election time. On the other side, he regularly farmed out rackets-related work to the Unione and Camorra foot soldiers, ensuring his value to both sides.

Gallucci could withhold as well as give. In 1913, Masseria

Right Place, Right Time

was back in court, this time for the attempted burglary of a pawnshop. Gallucci may have had the pawnbroker under his protection. He may have decided Masseria was becoming too aggressive. Or perhaps it was the leaders of the Morello-Terranova Gang that decided he needed to be reined in. Whatever the reason, Masseria, supposedly a rising star in the Morello-Terranova family, became a fallen star. He suffered a career setback: he was sentenced to four and a half years in prison.

Masseria could carry a grudge. Even before he went off to prison, he began breaking off good relations with the Morello-Terranovas. He operated more and more independently of the gang and withheld tribute as he did so. Masseria viewed their failure to "fix" his charge as a betrayal. Eventually he would take over the gang, using murder of some of its key members as rungs on his ladder to leadership. He may have signaled his break from the gang in May 1914 by shooting to death Charles Lamonti, an important Morello-Terranova ally. On the other hand, Masseria's involvement in the hit was only rumored — but the rumor was enough to ensure the gang would have no second thoughts about helping him out of his legal jam. The killing of Lamonti could also have been the work of ambitious Sicilian up-and-comers led by Umberto Valenti, who was contesting Morello-Terranova rackets hegemony at the time. But a third theory was the most likely: the Sicilians and the Italians were simply still at each other's throats.

In 1915, even Gallucci, adept as he was at playing both ends against the middle, couldn't escape the conflict. During the evening of May 17, "Don" Gallucci and his son, Luca, strolled over to inspect a coffeehouse the don had just purchased for his son. No sooner were they inside the door than gunfire erupted. Luca jumped to shield his father, but he was too late; the don was hit in the stomach and neck. Luca also took a round in the stomach. Both men died shortly afterward in Bellevue Hospital.

The *Washington Post* saw fit to run an article about the don's demise, naming Gallucci as possibly the richest and most influential Italian in America. The paper also noted that in the preceding year, as many as 10 of his bodyguards had died in defense of his life. Speaking to his influence, the paper observed that for two years Gallucci was free on $10,000 bail for a concealed weapons charge that hadn't even advanced to a preliminary hearing — a case that, in New York courts of the times, would have been wrapped up in 30 days.

Less than five months after Gallucci's death, Charles Lamonti's brother, Joe, was shot dead at the same corner where Charles got his. Throughout 1916, a scorecard was needed to keep track of who was alive and who was suddenly dead. Meanwhile, Masseria was doing his time, and biding his time. By 1920, he was out and about again, taking care of business.

Masseria's relations with the Morello-Terranova Gang remained cool. The gang had been weakened by arrests and killings, providing Masseria a vacuum that he could fill with his own loyalists while still appearing to be an obedient soldier. With that, he had a hard eye on ousting the gang from power, and Prohibition put him in the driver's seat.

On January 16, 1920, the Volstead Act came into force, forbidding the manufacture, transport, and sale of alcohol other than industrial alcohol. For New York mobsters, life was never the same.

Giuseppe Masseria moved quickly to the top of the territorial heap. Through an ally, Tommy Pennochio, he gained control of the Liquor Exchange, the district around Kenmore, Broome, and Grand in the Lower East Side. There, bootleggers could buy, trade, and sell the illicit liquor being distilled or brewed in Sicilian mom-and-pop home operations. By this time, Giuseppe was now Joe, and about to become "the Boss" — a man with his own outfit, a man to be reckoned with, and a man still nominally aligned with the Morello-Terranova Gang, only because it suited his own purpose.

The gang was ripe for a takeover. Masseria's bootlegging operations were its main money-makers, and money bought the loyalty of the foot soldiers. Masseria was, by then, powerful enough to swipe the leadership out of existence with one order. But he waited, wanting to use it as a stalking horse to rid himself of a competitor, Umberto Valenti and his crew. Events forced his play when Valenti virtually handed him the Morello-Terranova territory.

On May 8, 1922, Morello-Terranova gang leader Vincent

Terranova was murdered. By then, Masseria was running the central liquor exchange on 16th Street, a clearinghouse for illicit liquor and beer, as well as drugs and stolen goods. In that role, he did business with most of New York's gangs. Later the same day of the Terranova murder, the devious Masseria made his move, as if to demonstrate to his own people that he was now in charge. He attempted to shoot Valenti but missed, killing Valenti's bodyguard instead. He was apprehended at the scene but never prosecuted. With Vincent gone, Masseria quickly stepped into the leadership vacuum in the Morello-Terranova Gang.

Three months to the day passed before Valenti had his crack at Masseria. Joe the Boss was a creature of habit. He left his house at the same time every day, walked a block and a half down 2nd Avenue, and entered his offices. He departed the office for long lunches, then returned to work late into the evening.

One morning, Masseria stepped out his front door, dressed for work, a new straw hat shielding him from the early morning sun. Two burly bodyguards flanked him. The three men paused on the sidewalk. The sun was bright, sky clear, air fresh — but Joe had little time to sniff the morning air. From across the street, Valenti, a gun in each hand, opened fire on him.

One bodyguard dropped, dead before his face hit the sidewalk. As best he could, Joe began running — he had no gun on him. His second bodyguard went down. By then, Joe had made it to a refuge of sorts two doors down from his house, Hainey's Millinery Shop. He hustled into the shop with Valenti hot on his heels, shooting and shouting.

Inside the shop, Valenti continued to blast round after round at Joe, who was ducking and dodging between racks of clothes. Valenti finally cornered him, crouched behind tumbled racks of lingerie and nightwear. This was the time for the coup de grâce, even though Valenti could hear approaching police sirens.

But as he leveled his gun to end Masseria's life, Valenti realized his moment had passed — he'd run out of bullets. Valenti took off running. As for Masseria, he had received a fright and been made a fool of on his own turf. He didn't waste any time striking back. Three days later, Valenti was shot dead outside a restaurant.

This probably would have been a case of "same old, same old" except for one thing: the shooter was purported to be Charlie Luciano. This was the first time Luciano's name had come up in relation to a gangland killing, and it was an indication that Luciano was involved with Masseria. (Luciano's association with Masseria may have begun as early as February 1920. He may possibly have had a hand in the murder of Salvatore Mauro, a Masseria bootlegging rival. Nevertheless, well into the 1920s, Luciano remained his own man, working with Masseria when it suited him but not working *for* him.) In any case, the Valenti's murder cleared the way for Masseria to consolidate his power. The last obstacle had been removed.

To some extent, all connected mobsters were expected to be entrepreneurs, earning a living apart from their criminal associations. They didn't simply hang around pasticerrias and barrooms waiting for murder contracts. They also had to earn a living, and there were lots of jobs from which to choose — loan sharking, street gambling operations, pimping, extorting, burgling, stealing cars, hijacking trucks, armed robbery, arson for hire. Others were bouncers or bartenders in saloons and, later, speakeasies. Popular, too, was acting as runners, picking up betting slips and cash from small bookmaking operations.

Luciano was no exception in this regard. He had his own ways of making a living, but he was better at it than the average foot soldier. During the early 1920s, he was busily making money thanks to the Volstead Act. So, it seemed, was every other criminal in town, but many of them could operate only by purchasing their liquor from Luciano and his interests.

In Manhattan, even ethnic rivalries were sometimes pushed aside by the pursuit of liquor profits. Sicilians, mainland Italians, Jews, and Irish dipped individually and together into the depthless pool of demand for liquor. Availability and price were more important than the heritage of the people with the product. An example of this was the fast rise of Owney Madden after 1923, when he was released from Sing Sing, where he'd been doing a stretch of 10 to 20 years for being an accomplice to murder. Madden became one of New York's major bootleggers and part owner of Harlem's exclusive Cotton Club, one of the toniest nightclubs in the city. He would spread around his considerable purchases, buying from Joe Masseria, Charlie Luciano and Meyer Lansky, and Dutch Schultz, in that way ensuring his supply and keeping everyone happy. Big Bill Dwyer was another prominent bootlegger and club owner who practiced the same approach.

By 1925, despite losing a few years to the prison system, Joe the Boss could feel he was at the top of his game. After all, he had effective control of Manhattan. Any Unione Siciliane who worked did so at his behest, to the extent that some of their incomes flowed back to him. Even Frank Yale, the Brooklyn don and close Capone associate, always showed him the respect he saw as his due.

Of course Joe still had visions of acquiring more and more, always more — money, power, respect. He was no fool, though — he always watched his back. Unfortunately, 1925 was not to be a good year for Joe the Boss Masseria. Running up his back was an aristocrat of the Unione Siciliane, Salvatore Maranzano, on a commission directly given him by the most respected don of all. This Maranzano character was from Castellammare del Golfo, in Masseria's opinion a nothing village 40 miles up the coast from Palermo. However, Maranzano's sponsor, Vito Cascio Ferro, did give Masseria some pause.

Chapter 2
The Party Crasher

Some men travel the world to learn, others do it for the adventure, and some do it because they have nothing better to do. Then there's a select group who do it to escape the law in their homeland. Vito Cascio Ferro was part of this select group. By 1890, he was a man to watch in the Unione Siciliane, having built his reputation in Castellammare as a shrewd planner, resourceful manager, and ruthless adversary; all of that, plus he showed unswerving loyalty to the principles of the Unione.

Castellammare may have initially seemed to Ferro far removed in almost every aspect from New Orleans, where he landed in America in the 1890s. But the Big Easy turned out to be just like home. It already had a close-knit community of Sicilians. Just like home, the food was Sicilian, the first language was Sicilian, and the deep suspicion of law enforcement officials was Sicilian.

Ferro did well during his years in America, splitting his time between New Orleans and New York. In New York, he hooked up with the Morello-Terranova Gang, helping them maximize profits from their protection rackets. He taught them the principle of "wetting the beak," that is, bleeding the victim constantly but never so much that the victim ran dry. Better, he counseled, to take a dollar ten thousand times than ten thousand dollars once. Ferro knew his stuff.

Eventually in 1903, he was run out of New York by local police when he came under suspicion for the gruesome, headline-grabbing Madonia barrel murder. He went back to Sicily, where he climbed rapidly through the Unione. By 1910, he had become Sicily's acknowledged "boss of bosses," the so-called *capo di tutti capi*. However, Ferro never forgot his friends in America, providing them a strong Sicilian supply connection for counterfeiting in New York City, to say nothing of a near monopoly on imported cheese and olive oil.

Ferro continued to operate from Castellammare del Golfo, the Fortress by the Sea. With Sicily's criminal underworld in his grasp, he began to have dreams of Empire, of course with himself as emperor. He decided the United States — all of it — would be his first conquest.

Toward that end, he enlisted Salvatore Maranzano, an ambitious, proven Castellammare mobster by then.

Maranzano was much like Ferro. He obediently followed orders, his collections were on time, he was respected by those who worked for him, and he was appropriately ruthless when necessary. Ferro wanted Maranzano to work his way to the top of the American Unione while maintaining his loyalty to him.

Maranzano was a rarity in the Unione, an educated man. He studied in a seminary to become a priest before dropping out to pursue less lofty interests. How Maranzano came to leave the seminary and end up on the seamy streets is unknown. What is known is that when he arrived in Brooklyn in 1925, already 39 years old, he was treated with instant respect. Immediately, he was permitted to develop a small Brooklyn-based gang, accountable to Joe Masseria and made up primarily of other transplanted Castellammarese.

Ferro's grand plan would have taken many years to realize, but events in Sicily accelerated it, thanks to a force even the boss of bosses couldn't control — Benito Mussolini and his Fascists.

One of Mussolini's first orders of business was to destroy the Unione Siciliane. He appointed a hardnosed Fascist, Cesaro More, as prefect of Sicily. "The Iron Prefect," as More became known, diligently rounded up known Unione members and threw them in prison. Those who eluded the prefect's net went underground, hoping to outlast the Fascists, just as they had outlasted other conquerors for centuries.

Ferro didn't make it. In 1929, he was jailed in Sicily's

The Party Crasher

Pozzuoli Prison, where he later died, allegedly of thirst. However, his dream of Empire managed to live on. When Fascism was on the rise throughout Italy, and Mussolini was already declaring he would break the organization, many young mobsters decamped for America.

Meanwhile, Maranzano continued bringing more members of the Castellammare Unione to the U.S. to strengthen his position. These included the "three Josephs": Profaci, Bonanno, and Aiello, as well as Stephano Magaddino. All would eventually rise to become Unione bosses. In addition were other Castellammare natives: Vincent Manzano, Joe Magliocco, and "Trigger" Mike Coppola, top-drawer Unione members. This flow was augmented by a number of lesser lights to fill the Maranzano ranks on the streets. All of them were ready for work at Maranzano's behest, and none harbored any particular allegiance to New York's then-reigning bosses, Masseria and Yale, nor the reigning bosses in other cities. Of course, for the time being, they paid ostensible respect to these men.

Maranzano's power base in New York continued to grow, fueled by liquor and incursions into the protection racket, loan-sharking, hijacking, and labor racketeering. His loyalists had no trouble finding work, whether in New York, Cleveland, Detroit, Philadelphia, or Chicago. They were easily moving up the ranks of Unione factions — after all, they were experienced veterans before they arrived in America. Maranzano's influence in decision-making councils was increasing.

Crime Boss Killings

New York's Unione factions were the strongest in the country, and the nominal role of America's boss of bosses usually fell to one of the New York bosses. During the mid-1920s, Frank Yale held this post, one to which Maranzano aspired and which Masseria regarded as automatically his if and when Yale stepped down. Masseria was relatively content with the current status quo because Yale acknowledged Masseria's strength. In New York, the two were almost equals, Manhattan on one side, Brooklyn on the other. Meanwhile, Maranzano was biding his time. He had successfully planted his feet in both camps. Where he was active in Manhattan, he paid tribute to Masseria; where he was active in Brooklyn, he paid it to Yale.

Then Yale had a falling out with Al Capone, a clash of egos. As the presumed national boss of the Unione Siciliane, Yale expected tribute from individual bosses in the cities where the Unione operated, Capone in Chicago included. Big Al thought otherwise.

Yale's Brooklyn organization was Al Capone's chief supplier of imported liquor. Suddenly, Big Al's liquor shipments from Yale's warehouses on the Brooklyn docks, paid for in advance, were being hijacked. Ever obliging to his friend, Yale always managed to find more to sell to him. In fact, Yale was doing the hijacking, then selling the same load to Capone twice and sometimes three times.

Yale's technique was simple and usually bloodless. The easiest way was to take payment from a Capone emissary

The Party Crasher

at a Brooklyn warehouse, then have the warehouse raided by hijackers before the liquor could be shipped. The hijackers would then move the liquor to another Yale warehouse. Another method was to sell the shipment to a Capone rival or a Yale ally, such as Joe Aiello, in Chicago or one of the cities en route. For Yale, providing prospective buyers/hijackers with shipment schedules and inventories was easy.

By the fall of 1927, Capone took to supplying his own trucks, drivers, and guards for the NYC-Chicago run. At first his luck improved — loads were getting through more or less unmolested. Then, an incident on November 7 changed his luck dramatically. That night, just west of Fort Wayne, Indiana, nearly safely home in Chicago, his four-truck, three-car convoy pulled into a roadhouse for a meal and a few drinks before finishing the run. As most of the group went inside, a few of the men riding shotgun remained posted in the parking lot to guard the vehicles.

Suddenly, shooting erupted outside and the building was struck with an overwhelming barrage of gunfire. No one inside dared put up their heads, let alone return fire. In barely more than a minute, the shooting stopped, replaced by the sound of truck engines receding as the load disappeared east toward Fort Wayne.

When the dazed men finally trusted the quiet enough to poke up their heads and peer out the shattered windows, they saw a parking lot empty except for men lying on the gravel, and one car, clearly out of commission. The first tally:

two men were dead outside and one inside; four others were wounded outside and several inside were cut by flying glass.

It was soon discovered that the telephone line to the roadhouse and several nearby homes and businesses had been cut. The walk to a working phone was a little over a mile down the road. No one wanted to make the walk. More important, no one wanted to make the call to Capone to report yet another lost load. Bearers of bad news, apparently, had a short life expectancy.

Eventually, a passing car was commandeered and someone made the call. By then, the booze in the four trucks and two cars had been offloaded onto five trucks with Michigan license plates and was wending its way back along secondary roads to Detroit. The trucks carried a cargo that the Purple Gang (a powerful Jewish gang based in Detroit) could not obtain from across the Detroit River — Scotch from the British Isles and rum from the Caribbean. As a final insult, Capone's trucks and cars were torched in an Indiana stubble field. Frank Yale was determined to get his tribute one way or another.

At the time, Capone was having troubles on the home front as well. In his efforts to obtain total control of Chicago, he had engineered a split with the local Unione Siciliane, of which Yale was national boss. Capone wanted the Unione Siciliane in his pocket. He chafed at the fact that the Unione demanded tributes from him but provided nothing in return. Joe Aiello was Yale's nominee for Capone's replacement as top

The Party Crasher

dog of the local Unione.

Despite Yale's "lobbying," a Capone stooge named Antonio Lombardo was installed as Chicago's Unione boss, and he promptly opened membership to non-Sicilians — a sacrilege! Yale demanded Lombardo's replacement by Joe Aiello. Lombardo refused to step down.

In June 1928, six months after this confrontation, Capone and his underbosses met in Miami for an extended "vacation." On July 1, Frank Yale was shot to death in Brooklyn. Although no one was arrested for the shooting, ballistics later linked the bullets dug out of Frank, his car, and neighborhood houses to those dug out of the 1929 St. Valentine's Day Massacre victims. Clearly, Capone had tired of diplomacy.

Capone made that emphatically clear in May 1929, when, at a supposed celebration, he personally killed three defectors from his gang. From that point, Chicago's crime scene became tranquil, except for the uproar in the media. But Capone's actions were not viewed with approbation by bosses across the country. Between the St. Valentine's Day Massacre and the triple homicide, he was drawing too much attention to himself and the underworld.

Public outrage was at a new high in Chicago. A week after the "celebration" slaughter, a meeting was held in Atlantic City, where Capone was persuaded to cop to a minor charge, do a little time, and take the heat off everyone else. Capone pleaded guilty in Philadelphia to a weapons charge and received a negotiated 12-month sentence, which appeared to placate the public and the crime bosses in their respective cities.

In his guise as a mere underboss, Maranzano was not involved in the Atlantic City meeting. From the moment of Yale's murder, he had been busy consolidating his own position in Brooklyn, grabbing up Yale's former territory. Capone had unwittingly done Maranzano an immense favor by removing a key rival. Masseria, who fancied himself Yale's logical successor, was fortunate to hang on to some of the Brooklyn trade unions, thanks to Luciano's man, Louis Buchalter. He also held on to some of the Brooklyn docks, thanks to Genovese, another Luciano man. As for becoming Yale's successor, Masseria chose to appoint someone else — let a shadow draw fire.

Meanwhile, Salvatore Sabella, Philadelphia boss and staunch Maranzano supporter, was unimpressed with the Capone conviction. No one had let him know Big Al was going to court in his sphere of influence. Sabella assumed Philadelphia had been chosen in order to embarrass him. He would appear as a foil in Big Al's machinations, and it would appear that Big Al's reach extended influentially into Sabella's realm. Nose out of joint, Sabella promptly committed resources to Maranzano and relocated to New York to work with him, bringing along nearly a dozen of his men.

Back in New York, the rift among Sicilians was getting wider. Maranzano's power had been growing in the last half of the 1920s. Although he still served Masseria, he was fast

The Party Crasher

becoming an increasingly powerful servant. He had gained a reputation as a good man to work for. His rackets were lucrative and they were expanding. His earners were allowed their heads, and ambition was rewarded. As a result, Maranzano's number of soldiers in New York City was in the hundreds — not as many as Joe the Boss's, but second only. The Castellammarese lieutenants were also capable men, notably Profaci and Bonanno, a luxury that Masseria's hands-on brutal management style had prevented for his own operations.

Masseria was not blind to Maranzano's growing power. Not only was he aware of it, he knew that Maranzano's influence was all traceable back to Vito Cascio Ferro and that damnable backwater fishing village, Castellammare del Golfo — such an affront to the Palermo people! No question about it, Masseria recognized that Castellammarese expatriates, the Ferro family members, were the dominant factor in this apparent fifth column.

As early as 1927, Maranzano's people had begun pushing out of Brooklyn, picking up rackets here, allies there. When Maranzano gained control of Yale's major Brooklyn rackets in 1929, Masseria's situation was all the more aggravated. While Masseria still got a piece of the action, the people providing it now more often owed their loyalty to Maranzano, and only after that to Masseria. In some sections of New York, Joe the Boss was becoming only the boss insofar as Maranzano let him. Even then, Maranzano's men were disrupting Masseria's operations, albeit clandestinely. Liquor hijacking increased, for now it had been taken out of the hands of mere soldiers and was being orchestrated from the top. Maranzano began making inroads into Masseria's bureaucratic payoff structure by paying more to corrupt officials than the Boss did. Masseria's men began getting arrested and going to jail because the Boss's "grease" was no longer ample enough to save them.

Lines were being drawn in more cities than New York. Joe Aiello finally took over Chicago's Unione Siciliane in 1930. The post had been vacant for a time. Aiello's predecessor, Antonio Lombardo (Capone's appointee), had been shot to death in late 1928. In Cleveland, the Aiellos (no relation to Joe) had buried their opposition, literally, and were trying to forge a coalition that would exclude Masseria. In Detroit, Unione Siciliane boss Gaspar Milazzo had backed Joe Aiello against Capone, despite Joe the Boss's attempts at mediation.

The failure in the Detroit mediation was Masseria's last straw. Clearly, as far as Joe was concerned, the people from Castellammare del Golfo wanted New York and, with it, the country. Maranzano was their strongest leader. Masseria now saw that Maranzano had deliberately flooded the country with Ferro loyalists — to Joe the Boss, this harked back to Old Country Unione feuds between local factions.

At first, Masseria's greed had blinded him to Maranzano's grand design. Now, however, he recognized that he needed to assert himself. To not do so would appear as weakness — in the Unione Siciliane world, that was fatal, because

The Party Crasher

Maranzano obviously intended to swallow him.

Masseria was no slouch. He had loyal troops, he had generals, and he had faithful Mafia traditionalists throughout the United States. He also knew, as did Maranzano, that as New York City went, so would go the rest of the country. Masseria began to see that if he could overcome Maranzano, he would become the national boss of bosses — no one else would be left standing.

Chapter 3
Neutrality, New York City Style

Joe Masseria and Salvatore Maranzano were the Hatfields and McCoys of New York City's underworld until 1931. The two had Unione Siciliane ties to different factions in Sicily that had conducted vendettas against each other for generations, often for reasons long forgotten.

Masseria had risen to power by using force, Maranzano by finesse and cunning. In New York, Masseria built his power on the same coarse regimen of excessive violence he'd relied upon in Palermo, favoring participation in the most aggressive of the Unione's rackets, such as protection and loan-sharking. Within his gang, he enforced discipline cruelly and arbitrarily, often delivered by his own hand.

Maranzano, on the other hand, had earned Unione respect

Neutrality, New York City Style

and built his power in a Machiavellian manner. Infiltrating his people into other factions to sow dissension and outwitting his opposition in business deals, Maranzano nevertheless demonstrated a willingness to use violence, though in ways more calculating than Masseria's impulsive style.

Maranzano could speak five languages. Masseria could speak only Sicilian dialect and some basic English. Maranzano believed total power was his god-given right. Masseria had fought and clawed for every scrap he had obtained. He intended not only to keep it, but to expand it by the same violent means — they were the only ones he knew. Inevitably, caught between these two very different Unione leaders was Charlie Luciano and his interests.

Luciano's start on the path to power had nothing to do with the Unione, but a lot to do with surviving in America. New York's Lower East Side didn't have much to offer a nine-year-old son of an immigrant laborer from a small sulfur mining village in Sicily. School was free in America, which presumably was a plus, but young Salvatore Lucania (Charlie) was placed in the back of the class until he learned some English. At least out on the streets he could speak his own language. Soon he was there more often than in class, landing himself in reform school for four months for truancy.

By the time he was 14, Luciano was leader of a handful of other reluctant Sicilian "scholars." His gangs specialized in providing "protection" to Jewish schoolchildren who were constantly harassed by older Irish and Italian children. The reform school sentence increased Luciano's prestige in the neighborhood. He was acquiring a name for toughness.

About that time, Luciano met Frank Costello, an older Sicilian street gang leader from an adjacent neighborhood. He also met another boy who would have a major role in his life — Meyer Lansky. Where Meyer went, so went his shadow, Bennie "Bugsy" Siegel. Within a few years, the four men had combined their resources and moved on up from penny ante to minor to major crime. The foursome also increased in number, with each new recruit bringing unique talents to the mix.

Giuseppe Doto, known as "Joe Adonis" because of his good looks, was the first. Luciano then recruited Vito Genovese, Carlo Gambino, Frank Scalise, and Albert Anastasia. Lansky did his part, recruiting Louis "Lepke" Buchalter and Longie Zwillman. Not to be left out, Frank Costello brought in Arthur Flegenheimer, who soon became known as Dutch Schultz.

Luciano's crew was unique in New York. It was a melting pot of Sicilians, Italians, and Jews. Traditional enmities had no place in their activities. They still simmered, but they were left at the door when it was time for the men to plan their strategies. The group operated without a designated leader. Proceeds were pooled and everyone was consulted on sharing. Luciano, however, gravitated to leadership. He was the organizer with the capacity to identify each man's best talents and steer him to that cause. In effect, Luciano was the chairman with a knack for achieving consensual decisions.

Neutrality, New York City Style

Apart from their individual endeavors, by 1920 the Luciano crew was making a name for itself in protection services, small-time gambling, armed robbery, and burglary. They would also periodically contract to provide strong-arm services, acting as collectors for loan sharks and bookmakers. Still, opportunities were limited. That is, until Prohibition came along.

Prohibition didn't stop the flow of liquor, it only made it illegal. Indeed, later evidence indicated that liquor consumption actually increased during the Prohibition years, 1920 to 1933. Luciano's crew was ready. Soon they were providing drivers and guards for bootleggers' shipments. Bugsy Siegel particularly enjoyed this aspect of the work. Impulsive, violent, and quick on the trigger, he saw danger in every set of headlights, and he had no qualms about shooting first and asking questions later. The crew relied on Lansky to keep Bugsy in check, and most of the time he was successful.

Luciano's breakthrough into Prohibition "Big Time" came from two Jews and an Irishman. His first wholesale deal was with Irving Wexler, known as Waxey Gordon. Waxey was a major importer of genuine liquor. Rather than simply ride shotgun on one of Waxey's New York–bound loads, Luciano dipped into his crew's treasury and bought the load.

Shortly after, through Lansky, the crew was approached by the king of New York City gambling, Arnold Rothstein, who had an offer they couldn't refuse. Rothstein proposed to import shiploads of liquor from Europe and the Caribbean.

The freighters would lay by just outside the international three-mile limit, along the coast from Boston to Virginia.

Luciano's crew, Rothstein proposed, would be responsible for offloading the cargo of the freighters situated off New York and New Jersey, and distributing it to prearranged buyers. However, they had to abide by one condition: they were not to water down any genuine product destined for Rothstein's customers. Initially, that condition was easy to accept — Luciano didn't have resources to alter the liquor anyway. Business took off. Soon they were doing similar work for Big Bill Dwyer, supplier to many of New York's Irish-owned speakeasies, nightspots, and gambling parlors.

At the beginning of Prohibition, the local Unione Siciliane bosses had moved quickly to secure a liquor supply for what they thought was the primary market. They monopolized the production of the home stills found in many Italian and Sicilian households. Bathtub gin, rotgut, hooch, jake — the stuff had a dozen names, but it could not compete with the real McCoy in quality and profit-making potential. By 1925, if they wanted that, and a regular supply of it, the Sicilians, including Maranzano and Masseria, had to buy from Luciano and his hated Jews or, worse, from the Irish. Alternatively, they had to entice or intimidate Luciano into their respective folds.

In the last half of the 1920s, Luciano's operations were a plum by any measure. Liquor remained the mainstay. Rum Row was clogged with ships carrying Scotch from distilleries

Neutrality, New York City Style

in the British Isles, fine wine and champagne from France and Italy, rum from the Caribbean, and rye from Canada. The trucks were never empty.

However fast the current, the men around Luciano were too ambitious to simply go with the liquor flow. Lansky began making gains in gambling and bookmaking, exploiting his expertise with figures. Costello, working closely with Lansky and his people, took an interest in speakeasy and nightclub ownership. Costello also became the crew's "fixer" in charge of the "Buy-Money Bank," the fund set aside for bribery payments.

Dutch Schultz was making his mark as a master brewer, reputedly providing the best beer in New York City. Louis Buchalter had graduated from operating a violent protection racket in the Garment District to more subtle approaches — selling services and lending money to garment industry unions and manufacturers. Much in demand, Buchalter, in partnership with Tommy Lucchese, was on his way to controlling the garment industry.

Meanwhile, both Maranzano and Masseria watched. Luciano's maverick street gang of young hoodlums, many of whom were still not 30 years old, were doing better than the old guard. They were quick, they were smart, they were politic, and they didn't mind "disappearing" someone if he became an obstruction.

Maranzano was the first to make an overture to Luciano. He invited the younger man to a meeting, to which Luciano was accompanied by Frank Costello. The deal Maranzano offered was for Luciano to keep his liquor business but throw all the other rackets into a common pot — Maranzano's. As was their custom, Luciano's inner circle met to discuss the proposition. Consensus was that Maranzano would isolate and kill their Jewish faction, then take over the liquor business.

This was Luciano's view exactly. Add to that, he loathed Maranzano's pomposity. In his autobiography, *The Last Testament of Lucky Luciano*, Luciano reflected on that meeting with Maranzano: "All during [Maranzano's] speech he was walking around the room. When he finished, he turned to us like he was expecting us to applaud him, like he was wearing a toga and [he'd] just finished one of those big orations in the Roman Senate. That's the way he always made me feel, like he was Caesar and I was shit. Frank Costello and I just sat there and we didn't say nothing."

Rejecting the proposed deal had immediate repercussions, primarily new respect in Mob circles because Luciano had stood up to Maranzano. New friends emerged, each of them powerful in their own right. The Mangano brothers in Brooklyn extended their hand. So did Nucky Johnson, who controlled Atlantic City, as well as Moe Dalitz and John Scalise, who in tandem ran affairs in Cleveland.

Joe the Boss Masseria also became restive. He tried enticing Luciano next. To the extent that Maranzano's megalomaniac pomposity repelled him, Masseria's crudeness did the same. "Masseria didn't have the background," Luciano

Neutrality, New York City Style

later explained, "and the education of a guy like Maranzano; he didn't have no culture. So, between being short, fat, and having a round face that was first cousin to a pig, the words that came out of his kisser was rough and straight to the point. He hated Maranzano's guts and he knew that Maranzano felt the same way about him."

Luciano also rejected Masseria's offer. It wasn't much different from Maranzano's except that Masseria demanded outright that Luciano get rid of his Jewish partners, a point that, of course, was non-negotiable to Luciano.

Shortly after the Masseria meeting, Luciano suffered some setbacks. Several of his liquor loads were hijacked, and federal agents raided two of his warehouses. He had orders to fill and no liquor — his reputation as a supplier was on the line.

Fortuitously, Luciano got a call from Nucky Johnson. Johnson controlled in-bound liquor shipments from the section of Rum Row along the New Jersey and Long Island shorelines. He had a deal for Luciano that required a meeting. By the time he arrived in Atlantic City, Luciano had his own proposal, simply a quick deal for an instant supply. He needed an immediate injection of booze for his customers and figured Johnson was probably the only man who could satisfy it. Luciano was in for a surprise.

Like Luciano, Nucky Johnson cared about the bottom line. He believed that violent squabbles between rival gangs were counterproductive. He had worked hard to achieve neutrality in his business relations. They needed what he had, and, due to his overseas contacts, he was too strong for them to simply take it by force. If Johnson's customers had disputes with each other, he insisted they settle them outside his territory. Moreover, he was adept at playing one off against another. They all had to deal with him. If they didn't accept his terms, he wouldn't do business.

With Luciano, Johnson had in mind a long-term deal, rather than just a quick fix, which could make both their operations more profitable and efficient. Johnson would provide first call to Luciano on all his imports. Luciano would pay a premium, but in exchange he'd have a guaranteed supply. Johnson had access to enough liquor that even loss of a shipload didn't slow him down. A deal was struck.

Luciano's immediate shortage problem was no sweat to Johnson. As an act of good faith, Johnson provided details of a load coming in destined for Maranzano and Waxey Gordon, a pair of customers that apparently weren't on Johnson's A list.

Luciano's crew had to act fast. Two nights later, a tree fell in the forest. It fell across a back road in New Jersey, blocking passage for two trucks heavily loaded with uncut imported Scotch and bristling with armed men. The trucks lumbered to a halt. Ten men waited.

Luciano described the event in detail, which suggests he was on the scene: "Siegel started to shoot right away, and then Lansky opened up. One of the Maranzano guys was

Neutrality, New York City Style

bumped off and another was wounded, and the rest of them gave up right away. But that didn't do them no good because we took away their guns and gave them a good beating before we took off with the trucks." Luciano had solved his shortage problem and maintained his reputation as the man who could always deliver.

By the late 1920s, Luciano's strength in the underworld had grown to the point that both Masseria and Maranzano still wanted his operations in their respective grip, but now desperately so. For years, Luciano had jockeyed his way out of total commitment to either. He'd done business with both, always with a view to keeping them off his back, never putting himself in a position where he owed them anything. His nominal allegiance was to Masseria, to whom he paid tribute, but Masseria had no control over Luciano's operations. Although Maranzano was still regarded as an underboss at that time, he was no less a threat. The Luciano crew believed all along that if either Masseria or Maranzano obtained control of their operations, they would destroy the leadership — Luciano, Lansky, Costello, Adonis, Siegel, and Genovese.

In 1929, however, matters came to a head. Both bosses had finally lost patience with Luciano. Predictably, Masseria lost his first, summoning Luciano to a meeting at his office. Luciano's informants had let him know this was Masseria's showdown time. Despite this, Luciano and his crew decided that Masseria was the lesser of two evils. He had more soldiers than Maranzano and was most likely to win any conflict between the two. Moreover, Masseria was easier to read, his motives and intentions always obvious. To that extent, he was less treacherous and easier to manipulate. It was decided among the crew that Luciano would join forces with Masseria.

Luciano took along Joe Adonis to the meeting. When they arrived, Masseria was alone at his massive desk, the remnants of a gargantuan meal spread out before him. Joe the Boss began by suggesting there was animosity between the two men, a superficial "let bygones be bygones" spiel that didn't fool Luciano for a second.

The spiel completed, Masseria bluntly stated his previous demands. He wanted control of Luciano's operations and he wanted them voluntarily turned over to him on the spot — a somewhat reasonable demand given that Luciano was a loyal Unione underboss. Masseria then gestured toward several doors around his office, implying that if Luciano's decision was negative, gunmen were in waiting. Indeed, Masseria warned Luciano that he wouldn't walk out of the office if he didn't cooperate.

But Luciano knew his man. "With all due respect," he reportedly said, "that's not the way it can work." Masseria raged, but Luciano held his ground. He knew, and so did Masseria, that any war against Luciano's group would ultimately weaken him against Maranzano. Eventually, Joe the Boss calmed down long enough to hear Luciano's proposition.

In effect, Luciano set the key terms, the terms he'd

Neutrality, New York City Style

already worked out within his own group as an acceptable price to pay. He would maintain his non-Sicilian business contacts. He would also keep all of his liquor interests, but he would supply Masseria's outlets. Luciano demanded a share in Masseria's operations in return for putting his own into the pool. As a significant measure of Luciano's power, he insisted he become Masseria's number two man, with absolute authority in decision making, second only to Joe the Boss himself. Masseria agreed.

Luciano had no illusions. He'd harbored a hope that Masseria would now have the strength to beat Maranzano when open warfare broke out. Immediately after the meeting, he admitted he knew he'd been wrong. "He's too old, too fat, and behind all that hard front there's nothing left but a soft brain. It's only a matter of time," he told his people, "so let's use it the best way we can."

No time was wasted — Luciano knew Maranzano would not sit quietly by and watch forever. The short-term mission was to keep Joe the Boss happy. Dutch Schultz offered up four dozen speakeasies to the amalgamated operation. Frank Costello put his slot machines into the pot. Some of Louis Buchalter's loan-sharking was anteed in, as were the Lansky-Siegel protection services, one of the forerunners to what the tabloids came to call Murder, Inc. Most important, Luciano used his organizational skills to streamline Joe the Boss's operations. This planning and efficiency soon paid off for Masseria's foot soldiers.

But Masseria himself wasn't totally satisfied. He still hated that Luciano's Jews and non-Sicilians continued to be actively involved in his operations — but as long as they were making him money, he tolerated them. Chafing him far more was his lack of control over Luciano's liquor operations, which in 1927 took a quantum leap forward.

That year, the "Seven Group" was formed, orchestrated by Luciano and a wise, respected, former gang boss from Chicago, Johnny Torrio. The objective was to ensure uninterrupted supply and distribution of liquor to the exclusion of outsiders by creating an alliance of the most prominent bosses in the liquor business on the eastern seaboard. The men who gathered had the power to achieve this end, controlling liquor distribution into the most populous area of the United States. Luciano and Lansky were prominent in both New York and New Jersey. Joe Adonis held Brooklyn in his sway. Longie Zwillman covered west Long Island and northern New Jersey. Nucky Johnson tended Atlantic City and the south New Jersey coast. Farther north, King Solomon, who controlled the New England states, came down from Boston. Waxey Gordon, dominant in Philadelphia and its surrounding area, was also on hand.

Masseria and Maranzano were not invited to the meeting, nor did anyone ask their opinions. Others of the Unione old guard were also excluded. As far as Luciano was concerned, "their Thing" was not "our Thing."

In the Charlie Luciano management style, there was

no boss of bosses in the Seven Group. There were also no contracts, no arcane oaths of allegiance, no treacherous side deals. Rather, there was accord, agreement to achieve a common purpose that would benefit every participant. While each boss would maintain his independence, Luciano — the de facto boss — would provide the coordination. Within a year, 22 gangs, blanketing the entire east coast, plus Michigan and Ohio, had opted in.

Throughout 1928 and 1929, Masseria, who had no idea of the existence of the Seven Group, appeared to be losing his grip. He became more demanding of Luciano in petty ways, treating him as a vassal rather than a respected colleague. His petulance and narrow-mindedness were a constant source of irritation, but Luciano patiently worked toward his own goal.

Meanwhile, Masseria and Maranzano apparently focused their attention on each other, at the expense of business. Shootings, raids, and hijackings increased on both sides. Bodies began to pile up. It was no longer enough to simply hijack a load of liquor — drivers were now beaten and guards shot. It was no longer enough to break up a speakeasy — bartenders were now beaten and bouncers shot. And it was no longer enough to rob a bookie bank — clerks were now beaten and managers shot. Runners for bookies were crippled on the streets. Bone-crunching collectors for loan sharks had their own bones crunched. Fires in Mob-controlled garment factories and other businesses became as common as beatings in the dockside longshoring shape-up lines. Inevitably, the violence began to reach the Mob's higher echelons.

Through it all, the Seven Group remained clear. The sole purpose of the group was to keep liquor flowing — the members had no axes to grind and everyone in the liquor business had to deal with them. Quite simply, it was in no one's best interest to mess with the group. There were still hijackings, but these were compensated by high overall returns.

Luciano summed up these early stormy days: "All us younger guys hated the old mustaches and what they was doing. We was trying to build a business and they was still living a hundred years ago. We knew the old guys and their ideas had to go, we was just marking time." Not for long, as it turned out. The long-forecast war was imminent.

Chapter 4
The Luck of Lucky Luciano

Joe the Boss was a man who simply could never be satisfied. He had swung Charlie Luciano to his side, and within a short time, Luciano had increased Joe's profits. But the Boss continued to grouse — he wanted more.

In the fall of 1929, Masseria pushed the envelope once more. In a typical tirade, he threatened to kill Luciano if he refused to turn over his liquor interests. Again, Luciano refused. He also decided he'd had enough. After consulting with his council, the decision was made to approach Maranzano. Once approached, Maranzano set up the time and place. Joe the Boss was now promoted to first on Luciano's "had to go" list.

By then, Luciano could put only about 100 men onto

the streets of New York — not enough to go to war against either of the two bosses. Masseria's organization probably numbered 500 (apart from Luciano's contingent), and Maranzano's likely 200 to 300.

On short notice, a face-to-face meeting between Luciano and Maranzano was set up for the night of October 17. The two men were to meet alone at a warehouse on Staten Island. This was Maranzano turf, under the control of Joe Profaci. Luciano, on reasonably good terms with Profaci, decided the location was probably as neutral a ground as could be found anywhere in New York.

However, Vito Genovese advised Luciano against going alone. He suspected a trap and suggested Luciano contact Lansky for his advice. At the time, Lansky was at home. His wife was pregnant, and his marriage was in trouble because of her opposition to his criminal activities. Out of respect for this situation, Luciano did not call him. Later, Lansky would say that had he heard about the meeting, he would have fought Luciano to keep him from going.

By Luciano's account, Maranzano started out the meeting in his usual pretentiously imperial manner, "the usual crap." His offer was the same one he had put on the table at their previous meeting, years earlier. This time, however, there was an additional condition: by his own hand, Luciano must kill Joe the Boss.

Considering his present and future involvement with the Unione Siciliane — not just involved but actually heading up operations — Luciano found the condition untenable. Among its arcane rules, the Unione prohibited any number two man who kills his boss by his own hand from succeeding to the top spot. Luciano realized that, whatever his view of this rule was, there would always be traditionalists who had the power to hold him to the rule, if not kill him out of revenge or simply for being disrespectful to his boss.

Accordingly, Luciano refused the condition. By his account, he was then knocked unconscious and strung up by his wrists to a beam. Regaining consciousness, he still refused. Maranzano then had him beaten "with belts and clubs and cigarette butts." He repeatedly passed out, was revived, and beaten again.

Luciano later quoted Maranzano's incessant litany: "Charlie, this is so stupid. You can end this now if you just agree ... Charlie, if you do not do it, then you are dead." The beatings continued, systematic and thorough, by men well practiced at such things.

Hours may have passed. Then, with a last vestige of strength, Luciano lashed back, kicking Maranzano in the crotch. The elegant boss hit the floor, twisting in pain and screaming, "Kill him!"

Before it could happen, Maranzano regained his feet, grabbed a knife, and slashed Luciano deeply across his chest and face. Then he seemed to cool off. He held back his men, saying, "Let him live. He'll do what has to be done or we will see him again."

Crime Boss Killings

Luciano was cut down from the beam, tossed into a car, and, a short time later, thrown out on a side road, where he was found by a passing police patrol car. In hospital, Luciano gave police a variety of stories, none of them remotely truthful. Frustrated, they threatened to charge him with car theft, a bogus charge from which they later backed off. He required 55 stitches and spent three days in the hospital. The facial cut left a permanent scar, and from that night, Luciano bore a slightly drooping eye.

A week and a half later, just one day before the stock market crash, "Lucky" Luciano had recovered enough to go for a walk. It seems that Luciano was the only man more or less "taken for a ride" who survived.

Masseria bought the story that Luciano had had the bad luck to be mugged, just one of those things that can happen to anyone in New York. He could never have conceived that Maranzano was behind the beating — Maranzano would never have let Luciano live. Business continued as usual.

In 1930, breadlines across America were getting longer; the nation's failing economy was only getting worse. Meanwhile, New York City's nightspots continued to pack in the crowds. El Morocco, the Cotton Club, and the Copacabana did great business. So did a club that journalist Walter Winchell called "the New Yorkiest spot in town." The Stork Club was a watering hole for the rich and famous. One of its regulars was J. Edgar Hoover, head of the FBI. The Stork Club was perhaps the only place where Hoover could rub shoulders with mobsters who weren't in handcuffs. However, with tensions between Masseria and Maranzano growing increasingly strong, even the most flamboyant mobsters rarely showed up for a night on the town. They were keeping their heads low, lest they be blown off.

By this time, Masseria was importing shooters from other cities. Maranzano had "spotters" cruising the streets looking for Masseria's people and shooters on call 24/7 ready to dash out and kill them, wherever and whenever they were found. With apparently overwhelming numbers on his side, Masseria seemed to have the edge.

Despite chaos in Mob circles, at the Stork Club, there was always genuine, uncut Scotch and an ice cube to drop in the glass. Sherman Billingsley, the club's manager and part owner, had to deal with mobsters daily for more than the liquor, which of course came courtesy of the Seven Group. Not only were several of Billingsley's partners in the club mobsters, the club's supply of fresh fruit and vegetables, meat and fish, and even the laundry service were in some way controlled by organized crime. As for the ice cubes, responsibility fell to a Masseria stalwart named Gaetano Reina, whose position was as unique in the underworld as that of "the Artichoke King," Ciro Terranova, who controlled New York's artichoke supply.

These were pre-refrigerator days. About 75 percent of New Yorkers still relied on 25- or 50-pound blocks of ice in their iceboxes. Fulton's Fish Market, the fruit and vegetable wholesalers, as well as butchers, shopkeepers, and pushcart vendors, had to rely on ice blocks and ice chips to preserve their goods, and it was Reina who controlled New York City's ice distribution. Who got ice and who didn't was Reina's springboard to power. He could make or break businesses by charging exorbitant prices or simply by withholding delivery.

Ice distribution was a niche business, one of those that the Mob was expert at identifying and exploiting. As with other seemingly innocuous "ins," the hold on ice could be spun off into many other opportunities. For example, if a pushcart vendor wanted ice, he might be obliged to collect bets. A shopkeeper might be obliged to put a "ghost" on his payroll, someone who showed up only to collect a paycheck. And a trucking or wholesale company might be asked for "permission" to allow use of its facilities or equipment to transport or store liquor, sell stolen goods, or engage in any number of other criminal activities.

Except for beer and meat supply (operations run by Dutch Schultz), the rackets in the Bronx were firmly controlled by Reina, largely because of his grip on the ice business. In short, Gaetano Reina was big — a very important cog in Masseria's machine.

But Reina was also becoming a big problem for Masseria. He had begun negotiating secretly with Maranzano to transfer his allegiance and his operations to the Castellammarese boss. Such a move would simultaneously weaken Masseria's position and strengthen Maranzano's, so much so that it could tip the scales in the rapidly escalating power struggle.

Masseria had survived too long in the treacherous world of Unione Siciliane intrigue to be without spies in the Maranzano camp. He was quick to learn of Reina's possible defection and quick to act on the information. He immediately summoned Luciano.

Uncharacteristically, Masseria did not order Reina's execution, the traditional sentence for a traitor. Instead, he said to Luciano, "If I close my eyes to Reina, then Maranzano will win this war without firing another shot. You must keep Reina with me and I don't care how you do it, but do it."

If Masseria thought he was in a bad situation, Luciano's was worse. If Reina defected, he would not go alone. He planned to take a close Luciano ally, Tommy Lucchese, with him. Lucchese and Louis Buchalter were still building the loan-sharking business that was ultimately intended to gain control of the garment industry. For Lucchese to be suddenly within Maranzano's realm while Buchalter remained in Masseria's would have made Luciano's long-term plan impossible. The potential for millions of dollars was at stake, to say nothing of the money already invested. While Reina was a party to the Garment District deal, Masseria was blissfully unaware of it — Luciano had simply withheld the information. But Maranzano would be too sharp not to notice Lucchese's "extracurricular" activity and be aware of its potential profit. Nor would Maranzano tolerate Buchalter's involvement, not for a New York minute, because Buchalter was Jewish.

For several months, at Luciano's insistence, Lucchese had been urging Reina to hold off on his move until the Garment District could be secured. His pleas were falling on deaf ears.

As always, the Luciano group met to discuss its options. Secrecy was vital. Despite the winter cold, the men met at night, January 14, 1930, on a fishing boat off Oyster Bay, Long Island. Lucchese showed up late because he had been dining with Reina, who told Lucchese still more disturbing news. Masseria was planning to kill two of Maranzano's top men in New York: Joe Profaci and Joe Bonanno. This was information Masseria had kept secret from Luciano, information that Luciano, as Masseria's number two man, should have been privy to before Reina.

The puzzle to Luciano was why Masseria would take a pass on killing Reina but go after the other two. "To figure out a Sicilian, you had to get inside his head and think like him," Luciano would say. He was no stranger to the legendary deviousness of the Sicilian criminal mind — he had one himself.

There seemed to be only one answer: the hits on Profaci and Bonanno would be blamed on Luciano. So, too, would Reina's failure to defect. Maranzano would come after Lucky like a raging bull. Given the intensity of the all-out effort Maranzano could mount, he would probably get him. The scenario would work out perfectly for Masseria — he would deeply damage Maranzano's organization, keep Reina's rackets within his own, and, after Maranzano did his dirty work for him, take over Luciano's rackets, which he'd always coveted. And, if Luciano's efforts to keep Reina on side failed, the killing of Profaci and Bonanno would certainly frighten Reina into line.

Once Masseria's plan became evident, the Luciano group considered its next move. Never an example of patience, Bugsy Siegel immediately cut to the chase: "We're always wasting time. You Italians are forever chewing it over and chewing it over until there's not a thing to swallow. There's only one way to go — we gotta knock off Reina as soon as possible and Tommy [Lucchese] has to pass the word to Maranzano that it was a hit from Masseria. And we gotta make sure nothing happens to Profaci and Bananas [Bonanno]."

Gaetano Reina was one of the most highly respected bosses in New York City. He always gave his crew a fair shake, his word was his bond, and he respected the traditions. But it was obvious to the men in that meeting that if he didn't fall, others would.

On February 26, as was his custom every Wednesday, Reina had dinner with his aunt. When he left her house, he was greeted by Vito Genovese. As he waved to Genovese in recognition, Genovese shot him in the face with a shotgun.

The repercussions of this hit rolled through New York's underworld as violently as a Category Five hurricane coming ashore. Maranzano assumed Masseria had ordered the murder. Masseria assumed it was Maranzano, possibly because Reina was trying to back out of their arrangement, thanks to

Luciano's intercession. No one thought Luciano was behind it — precisely his strategy. Eventually, Masseria took credit, holding up the murder as an example of what would happen to anyone who crossed him. He also took the opportunity to blame Maranzano for meddling.

With Reina dead, Masseria appointed Joe Pizzola to head up the ice business. Unfortunately for Pizzola, who was generally loathed, even by many Unione Siciliane members, some of the business quickly drifted to Maranzano. Perhaps suspecting they, too, were on Joe the Boss's death list, two important Reina lieutenants packed up their rackets to go play in Maranzano's court.

Luciano instructed Lucchese and other allies inside Reina's crew to hang in, play along, and be patient. This was a huge order for such men. Pizzola was more impulsively brutal than Masseria, especially in his treatment of underlings. Apart from being excessively violent, he was not above stealing from his own men.

For most historians, Reina's murder marked the official beginning of the Castellammarese War. It had been a long time coming — two aging warlords duking it out in the name of tradition, ancient animosity, and, of course, personal ambition. In short, a war like most wars.

Chapter 5
Pick Your Poison

The media image of Mafia hitmen as cold-blooded, calculating, consummately professional killers is as absurd as the portrayal of Bonnie and Clyde as folk heroes. Mafia hitman Joseph Valachi described his first kill, in 1930, as a "masterpiece of planning." His assignment was a Masseria ally, Steven Ferrigno. According to Valachi, he and three other Maranzano shooters rented an apartment adjacent to Ferrigno's house and covertly monitored comings and goings for several weeks before making their move. When the big moment came on November 5, they dispatched Ferrigno and another man, Alfred Mineo, with shotguns — can't-miss weapons for a gang that perhaps couldn't quite shoot straight and that chose mess over finesse to get the job done. As for the hit being a masterpiece of planning, had the quartet waited a couple more minutes, while Joe the Boss, who was in the house, put on his overcoat, they could have had him, too.

Despite missing Masseria, Valachi became a bona fide, though lowly, Maranzano foot soldier, assigned as a shooter. Whenever a Masseria man was spotted, day or night, Valachi and his chums would immediately go on the hunt. They didn't have much luck. Often their quarry disappeared, perhaps having finished his drink in one speakeasy and moved on to another. Occasionally, however, the shooters got lucky, and the game was afoot. Running gunfights sometimes occurred, but only rarely was the quarry downed. Hit or miss, the gunplay created a high stress level among mobsters on both sides. That, combined with the caution it inspired, may have kept many of them alive.

After the Reina murder, all pretence of co-existence disappeared. Masseria was so obsessed by the Castellammarese threat that he put Luciano's liquor business and Jewish connections in the closet for another day. He focused on fighting the war on several fronts, including outside New York City. He ordered hits on anyone he suspected had Castellammarese links: Gaspar Milazzo in Detroit, Cola Shiro in Brooklyn, and Joe Porello in Cleveland, to name a few.

Milazzo was the first to die, and he was promptly replaced by a Masseria man named Cesare Lemare. Schiro reportedly paid Masseria a $10,000 cash tribute to take the heat off himself, but then he disappeared. Masseria didn't go looking for him. Instead, he put one of his own people in Schiro's place. Porello was also killed.

A hit was put out on Buffalo crime boss Stephano Magaddino, as well, but Magaddino managed to stay unscathed throughout the war. Although Joe the Boss must have known Magaddino was sending Maranzano $5000 weekly to aid the Castellammarese cause, Magaddino may have been safe for a couple of reasons. Foremost, considerable Canadian rye came into New York through Magaddino's Buffalo organization, and the main importer was Moe Dalitz, now a Seven Group member and close Luciano-Lansky ally. Second, Magaddino was a cousin of Joe Bonanno, and Luciano was still striving to keep Bonanno out of the line of fire. Bonanno had demonstrated reluctance to get into the shooting side of the war. Instead, he took advantage of his boss's preoccupation, reinforcing and expanding his own business — keeping with Luciano's preference for business first. Bonanno's immunity may have extended to his relatives.

Indeed, Luciano would have had a lot to say about which of Maranzano's people were taken out. Masseria's best shooters were tied directly to him. These included Vito Genovese, Albert Anastasia, Louis Buchalter, Bugsy Siegel, and Dutch Schultz — even early in the war, Masseria was relying on the non-Sicilians he despised and, in some cases, didn't realize it. Any hit he called for was first vetted and then assigned by Luciano. A few got by Luciano, usually assigned to the man he'd replaced when he became Masseria's number two man, a ruthlessly competent young killer named Joe Catania.

Masseria won the early rounds, but Maranzano and his men were still a force, watching the shadows and legging it after fleet-footed enemies at every opportunity. They caught up to Giuseppe Morello, a long-time Masseria ally, and shot him in his office. Masseria appointee Joe Parrino was the next to go, followed quickly by Cesare Lemare.

Reina's replacement, Joe Pizzola, met his Maker at the hands of disaffected ex-Reina loyalists, possibly as a show of good faith just before the entire Reina organization swung its allegiance to Maranzano. Luciano had told Reina's men to be patient with Pizzola, and they had complied. It becomes reasonable, therefore, to assume Luciano finally gave the order. The time was right. The transfer of allegiance now suited his purposes.

The death of Pizzola did not distress Masseria as much as the loss of the entire Reina organization to the opposition. However, he was somewhat consoled in the fall of 1930, when Al Capone, now out of jail, came through for him. On a pleasant September evening, Joe Aiello lingered, chatting too long in front of a friend's home, and was cut down by machine-gun fire in a classic Chicago-style gangland drive-by.

Despite the way it is sometimes described — a scorecard of casualties — the Castellammarese War was more than a matter of tit-for-tat murders on the streets of America. Foot soldiers on both sides were dying, too. Some estimates placed the death toll at over 100, but more likely it ranged from 50 to 60. Add to that, some mobsters may have died as a result of the everyday risks that came with the territory — stabbed by a prostitute or pimp, knifed by a drug addict, shot by a shopkeeper who finally decided enough was enough, beaten to death in a barroom brawl.

In other cases, the war may have been a convenient smoke screen for the settling of old scores. It may also have provided cover for ambitious but impatient up-and-comers to clear their way to promotion in the ranks, especially in an organization that valued murder as a cunning form of brinkmanship.

Throughout the war, Masseria and Maranzano strove to bankrupt each other. Ransacked warehouses, hijacked liquor shipments, and wrecked speakeasies became commonplace. Arsons and beatings in New York, bombs in Chicago — each city had its own approaches to destruction. Financially, both sides were hurting. Just as Maranzano was accepting donations from Magaddino, Masseria had his hand out to Capone. Nevertheless, the cost of the attrition was rising, and business on both sides was hurting. Only Luciano and his partners remained unscathed.

During the Castellammarese War years, Luciano's strength derived from his ability to grow his wealth as Maranzano and Masseria depleted theirs. The Depression was hell for legitimate businessmen, but for loan sharks, it was heaven. Luciano poured money into loan-sharking through Vito Genovese, who was operating on the docks, and

Louis Buchalter and Tommy Lucchese, who were operating in the Garment District, concentrating on loans to businesses. Through Frank Costello, Luciano was putting out loans to cash-strapped high-society types and other people in influential positions. These he often ostensibly forgave — in effect, they were bribes for future services.

Economic desperation didn't hit only the high rollers. The same despair was on the mean streets, and the poorest person on the block was willing to bet a nickel a day on a number. "Policy," as the numbers racket was called, boomed — Frank Costello and Meyer Lansky's brainchild. If that wasn't enough, Costello's slot machine operations — from their manufacture to their placement — spread down the eastern seaboard and into the Midwest. Everyone, it seemed, wanted to gamble.

Of course, even in the Depression, there was still some serious money floating around, and Luciano found a way to get at that, too — through Moses Annenberg's racing wire service. Annenberg had gone to the high-tech giant of the day, AT&T, and made a deal for an exclusive nationwide line. Over the line, he fed horseracing results instantaneously from across the country, from wherever the ponies were running back to horse parlors that subscribed to his service. This was the birth of off-track betting, and Luciano was in on the ground floor.

Annenberg, a former circulation manager for the Hearst newspaper empire, came into the Mob's purview in a typical manner. In the fierce, often violent, circulation battles among newspapers for newsstand locations in New York and Chicago, he hired some muscle, probably Buchalter's and Capone's people, who, given their labor and management expertise, were by then acknowledged to be the best in the business nationwide. In quick time, Hearst became the holder of the prime street corners. With that success behind them, plus their expertise and involvements in gambling, they were naturals for a partnership in Annenberg's wire service, and Annenberg knew it.

When Annenberg came up with the idea of the wire service, he needed money. He went to Al Capone, who likely put him in touch with Buchalter in New York. The idea was first tested under Capone's aegis in Chicago, and it worked. The one competitor, a man named Regan, unfortunately died when his car was riddled with bullets one night — Big Al always believed in protecting his investments. The potential of the Annenberg connection affirmed for Luciano the value of expanding beyond the parameters set by the traditionalists in the Unione.

Along with these many revenue sources, Luciano had expanded his outfit's mainstay — liquor. Rum Row continued to boom, although the 3-mile limit had now become 12 miles, and the Coast Guard had enlisted help from the U.S. Navy to turn off the liquor tap. With Albert Anastasia in control of the port, Luciano could still dock freighters straight from the high seas onto New York piers and unload them into his trucks while the Coast Guard diligently patrolled the water off Long Island and the Hatteras to the south.

Luciano and Lansky also had label-printing plants, bottling plants, bottle manufacturing plants, and distilleries in hand. Dutch Schultz still had breweries. Springing out of these were speakeasies, from the lowliest to the classiest, and naturally, where there was gambling, there was liquor. Thanks to the sage advice of Johnny Torrio, Luciano and Lansky were already laying a foundation for the end of Prohibition.

Meanwhile, money was tight for Masseria, but he maintained a sense his war might still be winnable. Devious as ever, perhaps to put Maranzano off guard, in late 1930 he put out peace feelers. Very likely he believed a truce would give him time to rebuild his resources.

Maranzano's response was brief and to the point. He wanted to isolate Masseria, leaving him to the undivided attentions of Luciano, his presupposed assassin. He informed Masseria that before negotiations could proceed, Joe Catania had to go. Catania was one of the few Masseria men who did not answer to Luciano and, as Masseria's number one bodyguard, he was the most important.

Of course, the justification Maranzano put to Masseria was quite different. He maintained that Catania was a bane to both their businesses — Catania had personally, possibly without Masseria's knowledge, been hijacking Maranzano liquor convoys and orchestrating raids on other Maranzano operations. In short, Maranzano was telling Masseria he had a maverick on his hands, inasmuch as Catania wasn't paying tribute. Men on both sides of the war were dead because of Catania's actions, Maranzano accused, and tens of thousands of dollars were lost. In effect, Maranzano demanded a head, and ultimately he got it.

Who actually handed it to him is unknown. Maranzano had already ordered a hit on Catania before negotiating with Masseria — and it had been active for several months. But, then, Masseria saw Catania as necessarily expendable if he was to obtain a truce. Luciano also had an issue with Catania — the latter was not happy that Lucky had supplanted him in Masseria's favor. To that extent, he was an ongoing threat to Luciano. Poor Joe Catania never had a chance.

On February 3, 1931, Catania was shot to death. He was 29 years old, not much younger than Luciano, but a lot less wise. He was a testament to the relative youth of many mobsters of the time.

Peace was not in Luciano's best interests, nor, for that matter, was it in Maranzano's. Even with peace, Masseria would always be a threat. Luciano opened his own negotiations with Maranzano, not because Maranzano was appearing to be the winner of the war, but because Lucky had his own agenda — he had to protect the loan-sharking and liquor operations. By this time, Luciano was also becoming much more comfortable with Maranzano's top two underbosses, Profaci and Bonanno.

Maranzano was especially enthused about this

rapprochement. The vicious beating he had administered to Luciano was paying off. He knew he had been excluded from the Seven Group, and he wanted in. He saw Luciano as his entrée, a man he believed he'd cowed into submission. Moreover, the entrée to the Seven Group meant more than a mere piece of the action. Through Luciano would come control of *all* of the action — Ferro's dream way back in the misty wisps of his history, but Maranzano's reality as his heir in America.

The deal between Maranzano and Luciano was struck in April 1931 during a face-to-face meeting in front of the lion cage at the Bronx Zoo. This time, Luciano brought friends to the meeting — Tommy Lucchese, Joe Adonis, and Bugsy Siegel. Maranzano brought Joe Profaci and Joe Bonnano. Luciano, because he knew he was the only possible route Maranzano had to Masseria, was in the driver's seat.

Maranzano agreed to guarantee the safety of all of Luciano's associates, including non-Sicilians, and to remain hands-off in their business interests. Treacherous as he had already proved himself to be, he undoubtedly had no intention of fulfilling his part of the bargain once Masseria was out of the way. Of course, Luciano knew this, but he proceeded with his plan.

On April 15, Luciano, along with Ciro Terranova and Vito Genovese, met with Masseria and described a plan that would end the war and eliminate the Castellammarese threat once and for all. The plan involved wiping out Maranzano's

Pick Your Poison

New York lieutenants simultaneously, then immediately installing Masseria men in their place, in effect taking over Maranzano's rackets in the space of a day. This appealed to Masseria's penchant for violence and, coming from the always cool and calculating Luciano, had the ring of feasibility to it.

The four men spent the morning planning an end to the war. Masseria, of course, was exultant to get a glimpse of the victory he'd longed for. At Luciano's invitation, the four men drove to the Nuova Villa Tammaro for lunch, arriving about 12:30. As befitted his status as the boss, Masseria was the guest of honor.

Where eating was concerned, Joe the Boss was more trencherman than gourmet; yet he could appreciate that owner/chef Gerardo Scarpato's efforts, as always, transcended any meal he could have obtained in his native Palermo. First came the appetizers, hot and cold antipasto. Then, for the four, a brimming tureen of minestrone soup, followed by fresh calamari salad with scungilli and shrimp. Full platters came, empty platters left.

Scarpato next presented his pièce de resistance: lobster fra diavolo with pasta. Freshly baked breads were replenished nearly as often as the wines. Finally came pastries and a demitasse or two.

Around 3:00 p.m., Terranova and Genovese excused themselves, pleading that their workday was not over. Joe the Boss and Lucky Luciano stayed on, convivial to the last espresso. Scarpato went for a walk, and Luciano excused himself to go to the restroom.

Masseria was alone at the table, the Tammaro's only patron. As fate (or great timing) would have it, four armed men chose that interlude to enter the restaurant and fire six .38 caliber rounds into Joe the Boss.

In the follow-up investigation, Luciano later pleaded, apologetically, that "the call of nature" ruled him out as a suspect. Scarpato would plead to the lure of a spring afternoon. Not one of the four men — rumored to have been Bugsy Siegel, Albert Anastasia, Joe Adonis, and Vito Genovese — nor their driver, Ciro Terranova, ever had to plead anything. They were never asked.

For Joe Masseria, the Castellammarese War was over. For Luciano, it was one down, one to go. Even though Lucky had clearly not pulled the trigger — a matter of hairsplitting except in the Unione — he had done Maranzano's bidding. For now, that was good enough to satisfy Maranzano, who presumed Lucky had pulled the trigger himself.

Chapter 6
Peacetime Plotting

The stature of a "made man" in life was often only measured by the grandeur of his funeral. In death, Joe the Boss was accorded all the respect he had sought so diligently in his lifetime.

The Boyertown Funeral Home in Brooklyn handled the obsequies. In itself, this was a measure of respect because, since the $50,000 Frank Yale funeral in 1928, Boyertown was the funeral parlor of choice for the big Mob send-offs.

Masseria lay in state for several days, giving out-of-towners enough time to get to New York to pay their last respects. Cars from the rental business run by Lansky and Siegel were pressed into service, providing complimentary chauffeuring of Lower East Siders to the viewings.

The procession to the Calvary Cemetery in Queens was

longer than the Macy's Thanksgiving Day parade — car after car bursting with flowers, limo after limo carrying the crème de la crème of the Mob, Masseria foot soldiers, Tammany Ward heelers, and lesser lights, all dressed in best black. Police patrolmen, happy to get the overtime, marched on horseback or foot patrols alongside the procession to ensure onlookers stayed on the sidewalk. Others cleared intersections, and a motorcycle contingent rode front and back. About the only thing Boyertown didn't provide was a horse with an empty saddle, a traditional symbol when a leader has fallen, though apparently not for the Unione.

Regardless, Masseria's spirit did not linger long over New York City's organized crime scene. To Maranzano, the death of Joe the Boss signaled the end of the Castellammarese War. All that remained was to clean out a few pockets of resistance and consolidate the victory. Primarily, this came down to Maranzano's people becoming highly visible in Masseria's former territory and, of course, making the collections and approving the deals.

With the death of Masseria, Luciano and his partners had accepted the fact that Maranzano would take the leadership spot in the Unione Siciliane and, with it, effective control of New York City operations. Nonetheless, they gave the new boss a period of grace. None were ready to go head-to-head with him at that time, preferring to wait for him to lay out his new regime's plans. Maranzano took the calm to mean all were properly intimidated by his power.

Peacetime Plotting

Luciano knew from experience that Maranzano would be obnoxiously pompous, probably more so than when his victory was still in question. Always studious, Meyer Lansky spent some time reading up on the Romans, particularly Julius Caesar. This seemed to him a good way to know his enemy. He expected that Maranzano would demand an "emperor anointing." Maranzano admired the way Julius Caesar had structured his army. According to Luciano's spies in the boss's house, he also liked the way Charlemagne had seized a moment and crowned himself emperor of the Holy Roman Empire. He would take these two and blend them with what Florida boss Santo Trafficante called "that Sicilian mumbo-jumbo crap," to fashion the style and substance of his new regime.

In order to do all this, Maranzano needed a stage. He couldn't very well lead a triumphant victory march up Park Avenue or through the streets of Brooklyn. He couldn't strut about majestically in a toga and a crown of grape leaves. He was obliged to select a more mundane setting, though when he was finished with the decoration, it was not so mundane after all.

To begin, Maranzano booked a banquet hall on the Bronx's Grand Concourse. The Grand Concourse itself was a spectacular Art Deco New York version of Paris's Champs-Elysées and Rome's Appian Way. Not surprisingly, it was also the main parade route through the Bronx. The limos arriving for his gathering were themselves a victory parade of sorts.

Everyone who received an invitation showed up or sent representatives, from the lowliest foot soldier to borough boss. Doubtless, to not make an appearance would have been noted and deemed an insult. Consequences of a no-show? Well, Maranzano was a proud, easily offended man who was stringently bound to tradition. To insult him was to insult history, and, accordingly, to invite swift retribution.

On the appointed evening, more than 500 mobsters from throughout New York City and many other parts of the country filed into the banquet hall. They were escorted to their respective tables, assigned according to their rank, with the foot soldiers, of course, at the back of the hall.

Maranzano waited in the wings for his grand entrance. There was, by design, no receiving line or head table where he would be obliged to congenially press the flesh or exchange banalities with vassals. He believed himself above that. Maranzano would arrive only when the various lords and their minions were seated and the first bottles of wine decanted into glasses. He knew one of the best ways to dominate a room was to not be in it.

He wasn't missed. The guests had lots to occupy their sensibilities during the first few minutes, notably the decorations. Said Luciano later: "... the whole joint was wall to wall crosses, religious pictures, statues of the Virgin and saints I'd never heard of. Maranzano was the biggest cross nut in the world — he wore a cross around his neck, he had them in his pockets, wherever he was there was crosses all over the place.

Peacetime Plotting

He was an absolute maniac on religion."

That contradiction to his ruthlessness may have momentarily mystified many of the more than 500 mobsters in the hall, but Maranzano himself was supremely comfortable in the setting he'd devised. The story is told that once, when one of his shooters had expressed misgivings about committing a murder one day and attending church the next, he had replied, "That has nothing to do with it. Religion is only concerned with a man's soul." After all, he had studied for the priesthood. He prided himself on knowing the ins and outs of religious rhetoric.

Once everyone was settled, Maranzano walked to his place — an elaborate chair from a theatrical prop store, a "throne," as Luciano called it, centered on a raised dais facing his audience. He then summoned the men who would be his designate lords to join him. They dutifully took their lesser seats to his right and left. There were five: Luciano (on his immediate right), Joe Profaci, Joe Bonanno, Vincent Mangano, and Tom Gagliano.

Maranzano began his speech slowly and solemnly, using mostly Italian, but slipping fluently into the Sicilian dialect to make special points or emphasize focused appeals. He was a slick, accomplished speaker, almost managing to not come across as a paternalistic despot.

He took his audience through the disputes of the last few years. He recounted past negative events, terming them corruptions of his vision for unity and peace. Positive events, like Masseria's demise, he described as his own ultimate victories over venality. He paced, he whispered, he shouted. His arms moved in emphasis and cadence like a symphony conductor's. He oozed patrician righteousness. Though awed by the trappings of religiosity lining the walls, he was no priest intoning a mass; he was a hellfire preacher bent on converting everyone in his tent.

Maranzano declared himself *capo di tutti capi*, the boss of bosses — this, for the good of all. In his wisdom and "humility," he saw no other way to bring peace, and that, he said, would be spread across all of America. The Unione Siciliane, as far as he believed, should be happy to have a strong leader with a clear vision, a unifier who would reach out to everyone and end the years of wasteful violence.

To start, he described the structure he would institute in New York City, the center of the Mafia and Unione Siciliane. There would be at the top, answerable to him, five *capos*. First, his right hand, Luciano, who would be in charge of the late Masseria's rackets and would act as Maranzano's overseer. Bonanno, Profaci, and Mangano would continue to manage their own well-defined territories, and Gagliano would be responsible for Reina's former holdings.

Not done, Maranzano then extolled the historical military successes of Julius Caesar, attributing them to Caesar's brilliance, not much different from his own, and Caesar's organizational structure, which Maranzano opined would work for the Mob, as well.

Peacetime Plotting

By this time, his audience was no longer mesmerized by the dapper don with the piercing eyes and receding hairline, though obviously the man had mesmerized himself. They were likely getting a little hungry and thirsty. Many knew the new boss was down to the fine points and hoped he'd wrap it up quickly.

But Maranzano continued. Each *capo* would have a designated underboss, beneath whom would be several lieutenants, the number dependent on the scope of the family's operations. Each lieutenant would be responsible for the soldiers beneath him, and these would be grouped into tens. The buck stopped at each man up the chain of command. This was Caesar's way, said Maranzano. So, then, would it be New York's way, and America's way.

Maranzano laid down five basic rules of order:

1. No man would ever talk about the organization to anyone, including his own family, on penalty of death.
2. Every man must obey, without question, any order of the leader above him.
3. No man must ever strike another member, whatever the provocation.
4. All grievances to that day, imagined or not, must be forgiven and total amnesty granted.
5. Total harmony was to rule business and personal

relationships between families and members. Moreover, no man could ever covet another's business or another's wife.

Maranzano had subsections to these rules. For example, in the matter of wooing other family members' daughters or relatives, chaperones were to be present at all times. After running through the remaining subsections, Maranzano finally commanded the banquet be served.

Over the course of the evening, the men in the room came forward individually to the self-proclaimed boss of bosses to pledge their allegiance. The tribute jars filled. Maranzano collected at least $100,000 that night, and some estimates put the figure at $1 million — all cash, all tax-free.

To exhort these men to put grievances aside, and to not covet another's business (or else) was naive, an indication to many that Maranzano was out of touch with reality. Bootlegging and gambling, to name two Mob enterprises, required expansion and alliances beyond the geographic boundaries set by the new boss's divvying up of territories. Friction was inevitable.

For generations, the position of boss of bosses had been more titular than commanding — now Maranzano wanted it to be dictatorial. However, to men who were more American than Sicilian or Italian, he was whistling in the wind of cultural change. Despite appearances, he won few converts that night. Actually, he lost some valuable loyalists. Moreover, the

Peacetime Plotting

war was not over. The summer of 1931 was only a hiatus.

By the time Joe Masseria was executed, the dimensions of the war had spread far beyond a factional dispute for control of the Unione Siciliane, whether locally in New York City or nationwide in all the Unione cities. When attrition left scant Sicilian troops on the ground, both sides were obliged to recruit Jews and mainland Italians.

During that summer, Maranzano ignored the Jews — no surprise since his anti-Semitic outlook had relegated them to the status of cannon fodder at best, ciphers at worst. But, just as Maranzano busied himself consolidating the Unione, the Jews were doing the same in Luciano's interests.

Within New York City's organized gang structure was a strong, active Jewish contingent. In the Brownsville section, for example, were the Amboy Dukes. Among its members were Sammy "Red" Levine and Abe "Bo" Weinburg. Then there was Louis Buchalter and "Big Greenie" Greenberg, Whitey Kashower, Allie "Tick Tock" Tannenbaum, Dutch Schultz, and Jake "Gurrah" Shapiro — all men who were as influential as the men in the Unione Siciliane and their mainland Mafia/Camorra cousins. Over in New Jersey were Doc Stacher and Longie Zwillman. Like those in New York, their loyalty was also assured. The Jews were all men upon whom Lansky and Luciano could depend.

If anyone had been paying attention to Meyer Lansky that summer — which they appeared not to be — they would have noticed he was on the road. One reason for this trip was to seek out medical treatment for his son, who had been born with a spinal disability. But Lansky was also meeting with business associates in order to dispel any concerns arising from the Masseria hit and Luciano's prominent emergence in the Maranzano camp.

In Philadelphia, as Salvatore Sabella was thinking of retirement after a long successful career as a Unione don (he was 40), an ambitious Jewish gangster named Harry Stromberg was looking for a piece of the action that might fall out during the transition period — the inevitable shakedown that occurred when an old boss retired and a new boss took over. Lansky spent some time conferring with Stromberg, spelling out the support and cooperation his efforts would obtain from New York.

As Al Capone was striving to get out from under tax evasion charges, his accountant, a former white slaver named Jake "Greasy Thumb" Guzik, and another Jew, Murray "the Camel" Humphreys, were quickly becoming more prominent and powerful in the Chicago underworld. Lansky dropped by for some "socializing" with them.

Lansky traveled as far west as Minneapolis-St. Paul to meet with Isadore "Kid" Cahn Blumenfeld, Dick and Mickie Berman, and Isadore's brother, Yiddy Bloom. Together, these men controlled much of the Bronfman Canadian whiskey flowing as far south as Colorado and New Mexico.

Then, of course, there was a stopover in Detroit to visit with the Purple Gang's Abe Bernstein, and on to Cleveland.

Peacetime Plotting

The Castellammarese War had wreaked havoc there, the factions having so decimated each other that Jewish mobsters who stayed above the fray, such as Moe Dalitz, Louis Rothkopf, and Morris Kleinman, were running the lion's share of bootlegging and gambling operations.

Waxey Gordon got a brief courtesy call, but by then, Luciano and Lansky were primarily interested in finding an innocuous way to get rid of him. For years, Gordon had overcharged them for liquor, shorted them on loads, chiseled them on shares in joint ventures, and tried to pass off watered liquor on them. They found the way shortly after the tour, when Jake Lansky, Meyer's brother, handed some of Gordon's tax records to the Internal Revenue Service (IRS). Gordon eventually went down the same ignominious road as Al Capone.

Lansky wasn't so much laying the groundwork for a Luciano coup d'état as he was smoothing any feathers that may have been ruffled by the Masseria murder. His message was simple: unrest costs money, ergo, if there is peace, everyone benefits. That had always been the Luciano-Lansky message. For a time, it also appeared to be Maranzano's. But during his travels, Lansky likely suggested Maranzano's message should be taken with a grain of salt.

Luciano could not move as openly as Lansky, but in the weeks following Masseria's death, he was able to reach out to a number of Sicilian bosses who promised support if and when a move was made against Maranzano. Some, such as Al Capone, had been Masseria supporters. Others simply wanted an end to the violence or suspected that Maranzano might take it into his head to come after them once New York City was settled away.

Santo Trafficante, who wanted Luciano-Lansky expertise to streamline gambling in Florida, came onside for purely business reasons. For John Scalise of Cleveland, business and personal reasons were deciding factors. The Castellammarese War had riven the Cleveland underworld, and some grudges were still unsatisfied.

Luciano managed a quick trip to Pittsburgh, where he met with western Pennsylvania's Unione Siciliane boss, Salvatore Calderone. Persuading him to join his cause was as easy as persuading Ohio boss Frank Milano, who was personally indebted to Luciano for past favors. Both, moreover, were dependent on the Seven Group for their liquor supplies.

Curiously, the bosses and their rank and file seemed to have a common trait. They felt there should be authority but hated to be ruled. Luciano's philosophy of the "non-boss" cooperative approach appealed to them much more than the autocratic boss of bosses school of thought.

As Luciano and Lansky worked to put their ducks in a row that summer, Maranzano heightened protection around himself. He traveled only in armed convoys and had increased his number of bodyguards. His days had only one routine — none. Appointment times and locations were changed even while parties were en route. His residences were transformed into armed redoubts. On one occasion, when he held a meeting near his farm outside New York City, he had an armed helicopter patrolling above. The wily old man even took a page from the Medicis, renowned poisoners of enemies, real and imagined: he hired tasters for all his food.

None of these precautions particularly indicated that Maranzano was becoming paranoid. Many were trappings he believed he should have as the boss of bosses. They were his due. However, Maranzano was behaving in a manner that eroded any credibility he assumed he had achieved. First was the issue of the money collected at the banquet. Unione tradition made such "donations" obligatory symbols of respect and allegiance. Tradition also dictated that the money be shared among the boss's personal lieutenants and foot soldiers. Maranzano didn't share a dime.

Another issue was around old grievances. The frequent liquor hijackings during the Castellammarese War had provided Maranzano a considerable fleet of trucks, many of which belonged to Luciano and Genovese. Despite his own dictum, Maranzano wasn't keen on amnesty and forgiveness if it cost him money. He decided to keep the trucks.

As for the dictum about not coveting another member's business, Maranzano appears to have taken a "do as I say, not as I do" approach. Rumors spread that he was hijacking liquor, raiding gambling operations, and stealing previously stolen goods from his "families." Perhaps he felt justified, seeing this as a way to counter any conspiracies that might be simmering across the country. If this was the purpose, it failed miserably. The conspiracies heated up.

Maranzano had picked up rumors of conspiracy, but did not suspect that Luciano could be behind any of them. He believed Luciano had personally killed Masseria. Given that, he had felt safe making him his right hand, co-opting Lucky with tradition — a man cannot succeed a boss he has killed.

Then, in conversation with Luciano one day, Maranzano reportedly said, "By the way, I never properly expressed my admiration for the way you handled the matter of Don Giuseppe. It was a very good job, Charlie. You should have arranged for me to have pictures of you pulling the trigger."

Incautiously, Luciano replied, "Even if you'd been there with your own camera, or sent God to do it, you wouldn't have gotten no pictures of me pulling the trigger. Like the newspaper said, I was in the crapper when Joe got it. So forget it."

Right away, Luciano realized he'd said too much. This new bit of news had stunned Maranzano — the "one time he couldn't think of something to say," Luciano recalled, "but I could see he was thinking and I knew what he was thinking about ... Me with a bullet in my head."

Until then, Maranzano had seen Luciano as a neutral, simply a man who had something Maranzano wanted. Now the boss of bosses realized otherwise — Luciano could be a major threat. In quick time, he learned of Luciano's conspiring with other Mob bosses and drew up a death list.

Peacetime Plotting

Luciano had as many spies in New York City as Maranzano, including several among Maranzano's closest people. Nevertheless, first word of the death list came in a roundabout fashion, from Philadelphia.

Suspicious about the presence in Philadelphia of Maranzano shooter Angie Caruso, long-time Costello confederate Nig Rosen set up Caruso with a woman, lots of food, and far too much to drink. The pillow talk was enlightening. Caruso bragged that he had a contract to kill Vito Genovese and another Luciano man.

Within hours, Costello had the information. Mere days later, Luciano had a copy of the complete death list, provided by a member of Maranzano's household. Bugsy Siegel was insulted when he saw the list. It included only one Jew — Dutch Schultz. Lansky, who always preferred the shadows, only smiled.

Further confirmation of Maranzano's intentions came to Luciano when spies informed him that Vincent "Mad Dog" Coll, a notorious Irish gun for hire, had been seen frequenting Maranzano's offices, obviously under contract to Maranzano. Such a high-priced specialist — his contract was reportedly set at $50,000 — would have been brought in for only one purpose: a hit on Luciano.

Given Maranzano's willingness to violate his version of Unione traditions, it's curious that he abided one and brought in an assassin from outside the families. Perhaps he realized that the New York Unione's ace assassins were all on

Luciano's team. In any case, the questions for Luciano were now when and how Coll would act. His response was already being prepared.

Maranzano's spies would have done well to have monitored the doings of Lansky's Jewish contingent. Had they done so, they would have noticed that in early August 1931, several members had dropped out of sight. Where they had gone and what they were doing were known to only a handful — Luciano, Lansky, Costello, Genovese, Adonis, Siegel, all the usual suspects. Something was in the wind.

Chapter 7
Checkmate

New York City's Grand Central Station officially opened on February 2, 1913, part of a magnificent "city within a city" between 42nd and 50th streets along Park Avenue, though it wouldn't be completed until $80 million had been invested and 14 more years had passed. In the process, 180 buildings were demolished, even churches and hospitals, but progress was on the march. Swanky apartment complexes, chic stores, sumptuous office buildings, and elegant hotels were built in their stead. This area, known as Terminal City, was the place to be for the rich, the famous, and the powerful. It was no surprise then that in 1930, Salvatore Maranzano leased offices for his Eagle Building Corporation in Terminal City — in the Grand Central building, the heart of upscale New York. In his view, he should be nowhere else.

Others, including investigators from the IRS, had different ideas. Certainly in Chicago, the IRS had shown its muscle enough to back even Al Capone to the wall. South of New York City, Waxey Gordon was discovering to his dismay that IRS auditors were not the average bribable public servants.

The IRS was also probing the books of Eagle Building Corporation. Again, reportedly, Jake Lansky had put them on the case. But this time, the reason was far more devious and deadly than a tax evasion charge against Maranzano sometime in the future.

Lansky and Luciano knew that any investigation of Eagle Building Corporation would come up empty. The company was Maranzano's blue chip plum of legitimacy. When the IRS came knocking, the boss always graciously opened the door. The IRS agents were provided every record they requested whenever they wanted to scrutinize files, trace paper trails, and do whatever else they chose while on the premises. Maranzano had instructed his staff to be deferential and helpful at all times. He himself was far more obsequious than any obliging American citizen and taxpayer needed to be.

Maranzano's smarmy approach to the feds appeared to be working wonders. As the summer of 1931 drew to a close, the IRS agents still arrived with stern looks; however, they invariably left with smiles and handshakes. But they still watched. Maranzano was confident his Sicilian cunning was winning out, always a move or two ahead of the opposition.

Checkmate

The master players of the game, however, were across town. Maranzano and the IRS agents were pieces on their chessboard. The agents were pawns being used to lay bare the vulnerability of Maranzano, the king — and the Luciano-Lansky group was determining the moves.

As it turned out, the Luciano-Lansky plan for the elimination of Maranzano was in motion before the boss of bosses had even drafted his death list or thought to hire Coll. Luciano had reached out to Lansky to orchestrate what was to be the most important assassination in the history of organized crime in America to date. The business of the IRS auditors pestering Maranzano was Lansky's opening move.

Both men realized that Maranzano was almost inaccessible. His schedule was deliberately erratic, his residences fortresses, and his bodyguards consummately professional. Moreover, between Maranzano himself and his bodyguards, they knew every Sicilian and Italian shooter within a thousand miles. Theirs, after all, was a small world — too small to accommodate Jews. In short, they were outside Maranzano's box.

As a result, it was decided early on that Lansky's Jewish shooters would deal with Maranzano — they would be unknown to his people. Even as Luciano and Lansky were courting support inside and outside New York City, four seasoned killers and their assigned driver had gone into seclusion. Three were imports, coming from Baltimore, Philadelphia, and Boston. Lansky was a careful man — he wanted no leaks beforehand and no identifications after. The fourth man, their leader, was Red Levine, a proficient killer so loyal to Lansky that he often used Levine as a personal bodyguard and chauffeur.

The four shooters were tucked into a Bronx house. There, for much of August 1931, they lived in isolation, not even stepping into the yard. Instead, they were immersed in the life and times of Salvatore Maranzano: his history, physical appearance, habits, homes, and offices; the people around him; what he ate, where he ate, and when he ate — every habit gleaned by Luciano's spies in the months of watching and listening.

In addition, the four were trained in the prototypical habits and demeanor of federal agents. Historians disagree on who provided this facet of their curriculum. Both Bugsy Siegel and Meyer Lansky have been named by some, but the more likely tutors were Frank Costello or Jake Lansky. As "fixers," both had had many face-to-face dealings with federal law enforcement. They knew their style and language — the walk and the talk. The tutors even provided cheap, ill-fitting, off-the-rack suits, topcoats, and shapeless fedoras from an assembly line tailor shop in Brownsville. Such was the wear of law enforcement plainclothes agents who did not take bribes.

By the end of August, the four were prepared. Genovese was all for ordering them into action, especially with Coll in the picture. Luciano wanted to wait a little longer to find out what Maranzano had in mind. Eventually he learned the details of Maranzano's assassination plan.

Checkmate

It turned out to be simplicity itself. To lull suspicion, Maranzano planned to summon Luciano and Genovese to a business conference at his offices, a common occurrence. This time, however, instead of meeting Maranzano, the pair would be confronted by Coll, who would gun them down.

Luciano didn't need to know the fine points of the plot, such as where Maranzano's legitimate staff would be or how the murders would be explained to police. He had enough information to act. Now he had only to wait for the right time. He knew it would be soon.

Finally, on September 9, Maranzano made his call, summoning Luciano and Genovese to a meeting at 3:00 the next afternoon. This was it.

That night, the Jewish hit team was introduced briefly to Tommy Lucchese, who would ensure Maranzano would be present, and, to ensure no mistake, be present himself to finger him.

Shortly before 2:00 p.m. on September 10, Eagle Building Corporation received several unexpected visitors. First among them was Tommy Lucchese, who had called ahead and come by to discuss an urgent matter regarding the Gagliano family. Almost on his heels were four men who flashed badges, identifying themselves as federal agents. Maranzano, who was in the reception area talking to Lucchese, greeted them with his usual charm, no doubt somewhat irritated by the notion that they might hang around too long and foil his 3:00 plan.

Maranzano was saved from the dilemma. In accordance

with the script he hadn't written, one of the so-called agents — probably Levine — demanded Maranzano identify himself. The room was crowded. Along with Lucchese, the four hit men, and Maranzano were five Maranzano bodyguards and the secretary, Grace Samuels. Maranzano didn't have to identify himself — a shift of Lucchese's eyes was all Levine needed. Notwithstanding that, Levine had already recognized his prey from photographs.

Two of the agents immediately steered Maranzano to his inner office and closed the door. The remaining two produced guns, disarmed the bodyguards, and lined up everyone against the wall.

Behind the closed door, the assassins first attacked Maranzano with knives, striving to keep the murder as quiet as possible. Maranzano fought back, even though he'd sustained six stab wounds and had his throat cut. To put an end to the desperate struggle, the assassins pulled guns and shot the boss four times in his head and body.

The killers then fled the building, rushing down the stairs rather than waiting for an elevator. One look at the carnage in their boss's office and the bodyguards also ran down the stairs, meeting Coll on his way up to kill Luciano and Genovese. One bodyguard paused only long enough to tell Coll what had happened. Mad Dog also made himself scarce.

Lucchese, the last man to leave the office, confirmed for himself that Maranzano was dead. Then, moments before

Checkmate

the police arrived, he leisurely rode the elevator to street level and disappeared into the crowd, just another businessman in Terminal City heading for an afternoon appointment. What became of Grace Samuels is unknown.

Meanwhile, Luciano and his key people impatiently hung by their telephones. Less than an hour after the murder, Frank Costello got the first confirmation from a policeman on the pad in the 53rd Street precinct. Later, Levine and Lucchese checked in for debriefing.

According to internationally acclaimed criminologist Donald Cressey, a second phase to Luciano's plan was then put into place. Known as "the Night of the Sicilian Vespers," this phase, implemented across the country, consisted of the execution of at least 40 pro-Maranzano mobsters to complete the coup. Cressey wasn't alone in his pronouncement that the fateful night had occurred. In 1975, Pulitzer Prize–winning investigative journalist David Chandler went so far as to estimate that logistically at least 300 Luciano allies outside New York City had to be privy to the plan for it to have worked. He argued that most of the bodies were found months after the bloody night, and the remainder simply never found. These allegations made great reading even decades later, especially when the theories were presented by a reputable academic and a professional journalist. On its best day, however, the Mob wasn't that efficient or close-mouthed.

In his memoir, Luciano pooh-poohed the notion:

Plenty of people got eliminated before the day Maranzano got his, and it was all part of the plan. But all that stuff them writers always printed about what they called "The Night of the Sicilian Vespers" was mostly pure imagination. Every time somebody else writes about that day, the list of guys who was supposed to have got bumped off gets bigger and bigger. But the funny thing is, nobody could ever tell the names of the guys who got knocked off the night Maranzano got his.

I, personally, don't know the name of one top guy in the Maranzano group in New York or Chicago or Detroit or Cleveland or nowhere who got rubbed out to clear the deck. It just wasn't necessary because what we did was to tell them the truth — that the real and only reason Maranzano got his was so that we could stop the killing.

In 1976, University of Kentucky history professor Humbert Nelli researched the issue in 14 American cities. He found that in New York on September 10, only three known mobsters, other than Maranzano, met their demise. Two were found in the Hackensack River and one was shot down in the Bronx. As well, there was a Mob killing in November, which, at a stretch, could be linked to events in New York

Probably coincidentally, September 10 was the day that Gerardo Scarpato of the Nuova Villa Tammaro Restaurant

Checkmate

was killed. His body was found stuffed in the trunk of a stolen car. The murder went unsolved. Maranzano's murder, of course, also remained officially unsolved.

In the Mob tradition, despite that he had become more loathed than Joe the Boss Masseria, Maranzano was accorded a fine funeral. Floral tributes poured in from across the country. Meticulously polished, the black limousines of New York City were on hand to transport the elite of America's crime ranks to Maranzano's final resting place in the Mob's "Boot Hill," St. John's Cemetery in Queens.

Luciano took time out for Maranzano's funeral. Lansky didn't — there were travel arrangements to book and a convention in Chicago to plan. Luciano wanted the gathering of crime bosses to take place outside New York. Although New York was the acknowledged hub of the organization, he wanted no taint from the Maranzano "coronation" attached to his own ascension. Moreover, he wanted to impress on everyone the national scope of his vision.

Al Capone was fading fast, but he could still command presence. Lucky persuaded him to organize the convention, appealing to his sense of self-importance and, of course, to his place as a primo heavyweight in America's pantheon of crime lords.

Chapter 8
Crime Pays

Whether by gun or knife, it takes a lot to kill a human being. Most people are reluctant to die. Maranzano had fought his attackers, but undoubtedly he knew that if he overwhelmed the two in his office, there were still more waiting outside. To his credit, perhaps a measure of the fear he'd created, he was not shot straight in the face, the traditional Unione Siciliane death. The head shot had come later in the melee. But the job was done and Maranzano was dead: long live the king. So who was the king now?

Luciano's answer to that question would startle the Unione Siciliane bosses who didn't know him well. The war was now definitely over. Both of its chief players were dead, and Luciano seemed to have control of the New York City rackets. Yet, he told the bosses, there would not be a *capo di tutti capi*. "That's nuts" was the refrain among the bosses. "He won, he's the boss. There always has to be a boss."

Within days of Maranzano's death, however, the new regime was up and running in New York City. It was business as usual — so usual that many could not believe anything had changed. The Five Families were intact. Even Castellammare natives, including Joe Profaci and Joe Bonanno, were still on the job. The Five Families of New York had been conceived by Maranzano, with all of them responsible to him as the boss of bosses. In effect, the five split New York City into geographic territories.

Across the country, the jury was still out on Luciano. Few were saddened to have Maranzano gone, but now they wanted to know what Luciano had in store. Some bosses had never even met him. They awaited his summons to New York for an audience. He didn't summon them. Instead, to show respect, he went to them, choosing Chicago as the city for the national meeting.

For a brief, almost euphoric period, Al Capone put aside his grief with the tax man and played the lavish host. Most who were invited to the event thought it would be about the same as Maranzano's — a coronation that, with luck, might have shorter speeches and fewer crosses adorning walls and shelves.

Capone booked two hotels and had them cordoned off from curious spectators and media. Police were hired to provide perimeter security. Inside, he assigned floors, rooms, and suites to the "delegates" in hierarchical order. No one would feel slighted by his arrangements.

On the day of the scheduled plenary banquet, Luciano used the afternoon to meet privately with many leaders, at which time he laid out his reasoning and his plan for the future.

Each local organization would maintain its independence within its existing jurisdiction. However, there would now be a national Commission made up of the most important leaders. As a group, they would set national policy and settle any disputes that arose between bosses before another shooting war started. Luciano would act as chairman of the Commission but, like every other member, would have only one vote. (In actuality, Maranzano had come up with a similar idea but didn't have time to implement it. He likely would have met resistance outside New York because he held to the idea that the boss of bosses had the absolute power of veto in all matters.)

Most who listened were pleased. Some, as Lansky pointed out to Luciano before the banquet, were puzzled. "There are lot of guys who aren't able to give up all of the old ways so fast," Lansky explained. "You've got to give the new setup a name. A guy doesn't walk into a car showroom and say, 'I'll take that car over there, the one without a name.'" They chose a name that would comfort the old guard: Unione Siciliane. Sure enough, on this point Luciano placated his audience.

Crime Pays

Nevertheless, he still had a few more surprises up his sleeve. To de-emphasize the assumption that the much-vaunted Unione Siciliane was an ethnically exclusive club in control of crime far and wide, and to emphasize instead that the audience represented powerful Jewish and Anglo rackets leaders as well, Luciano distributed these men in the more prominent tables at the banquet.

Lansky, Siegel, Buchalter, Stacher, Dutch Schultz, and Jake Guzik were only a few of the Jewish powers present. Frank Erickson, gambling's number one man in the country — former right-hand man to Arnold Rothstein — was also there. Big Bill Dwyer was on hand, too, as were two African Americans who ran policy for Frank Costello in New York's black neighborhoods.

For the first time at one of these gatherings, the Italians and Sicilians were not alone. Wide business interests, many of which were already at the table in day-to-day business transactions, were now acknowledged to be fundamentally of the same ilk. This mix impressed upon everyone the importance Luciano attached to their participation, and Luciano underscored this with an announcement.

Within his new structure would be a dispute mechanism in every family. A consigliere would act as an advisor to the boss and a mediator in disputes within local organizations. Moreover, the consigliere would be considered immune from reprisal, whatever his advice or decisions. As his own consigliere, Luciano then appointed "the Little Man,"

Meyer Lansky, a Jew. The message of peace and tolerance in this appointment was emphatic.

Luciano still wasn't finished surprising his audience. The moment arrived for the leaders to come forward with their traditional cash tributes. Although Luciano had told everyone he wasn't the boss of bosses, they weren't completely convinced — yet. Now he did something that convinced them he was good on his word, shocking even Capone. He refused the money, saying to each, "Why should you be paying anything to me when we are all equals?"

While Luciano eschewed the title, no one who left the banquet doubted he was, in reality, the boss in much the same manner he'd become leader of the Seven Group. However, questions remained. Would Luciano's proposed structure work? Would the killings stop? Could the Commission actually impose its dicta nationwide?

To the first question, the answer proved to be a resounding yes. The structure Luciano put in place, although weakened in recent years, remains today, still wetting its beak in the arteries and veins of American life. This, more than any other factor, made the Castellammarese War and Maranzano's murder very important to the history of American organized crime.

The answer to the second question was no, the killings did not stop. But most of them were more selective. The majority had to be sanctioned by the Commission, which in turn was reputed to have its own national enforcement arm, labeled by some law enforcement and media people as Murder, Inc.

Murder, Inc. wasn't listed on the New York Stock Exchange Big Board. No one owned shares. Rather, it was a fee-for-service, ad hoc, motley collection of murderers who most often took their contracts from either Albert Anastasia or Louis Buchalter. These men were a mix of Sicilians and Jews who were ready, willing, and able to take contracts anywhere in the country. Such men had always been a part of the underworld, but now, like crime itself, they were a little more organized.

As for the third question, with such a crew of proficient heavy hitters, few wanted to argue with the Commission. Dutch Schultz was one of these few, when he decided he would kill crimebuster Thomas Dewey against the Commission's express orders. The Dutchman died in the restroom of the Palace Chop House in New Jersey, shot dead.

Between 1932 and the end of 1935, with Luciano at the helm, organized crime in America entrenched itself in the national economy. The Mob didn't so much go after the heart of the economy. Instead, they continued to "wet their beaks" at the pleasure centers, notably the ones that stimulated the impulse to gamble.

New York City, more often than not, was where new schemes were tested. Gambling houses — the horse parlors and slightly more upscale carpet joints — were fashioned in New York and New Jersey. The "lake houses" of Saratoga

Crime Boss Killings

Springs every August became the forerunners of glitzy casinos in Cuba, the Bahamas, and Las Vegas. They set the standard. Then there was the numbers racket, slot machines in bars, even jukeboxes, until they fell out of fashion.

The transportation industry was where the Mob most lucratively wet its beak. They controlled the New York docks — 650 miles of waterfront. Lessons learned on its piers, in its union halls, and in shipping company offices were shared through the Commission. Before 1935, its influence was felt in every major port along the East Coast and Great Lakes.

Trucking fell into the sphere of influence, once more through unions, notably the Teamsters. From there, they expanded into industries and public services that were dependent on trucks, from food supply to garbage collection, from construction materials delivery to snow removal. In some cases, control of the unions unilaterally led to control of the business themselves.

This control shift also occurred within New York's garment industry. Controlling material supply and the labor force, Mob loan sharks and protection racketeers ended up controlling the business, just as Luciano had planned and Lucchese and Buchalter had executed.

Had it not been for the Castellammarese War, the end of Prohibition, in February 1933, would have gone far toward reducing the power of the Unione Siciliane. Very few local bosses had the vision on their own to diversify criminal activities, but Charlie Luciano did. The war cleared the decks of "old thinking." Had this not occurred, the Unione would have gone back to its neighborhood enclaves, wrapped again in the shrouds of narrow xenophobia that had characterized it before Prohibition. It was Luciano's guidance that ensured other bosses across the country would be prepared for a smooth transition.

In 1936, Luciano was imprisoned for living off the avails of prostitution. The charge was not totally bogus — he did control much of Manhattan's prostitution — but the evidence in his case was less than reliable. Shortly after World War II he was deported to Italy. Such was his power, however, that he continued to influence the Commission not only from prison, but from Italy in the late 1950s. Throughout the years, many of his staunchest allies during the Castellammarese War rose to become powerful Unione Siciliane leaders in their own right — Frank Costello, Vito Genovese, Carlo Gambino, and Joe Bonanno, to name a few. Others, such as Albert Anastasia, fell victim to the old ways — multiple gunshots.

The Commission, the Unione Siciliane, the Black Hand, Camorra, La Cosa Nostra, the Mafia, or, as Luciano called it, "the outfit," was, as far as law enforcement figures and politicians saw it and presented it to the public, a highly organized, nationwide, criminal corporation.

Epilogue

Both Joe Masseria and Salvatore Maranzano gave fatal disregard to the independent interests of Lucky Luciano and the like-minded men who orchestrated the Castellammarese War by clandestinely feeding the passions of the two old dons. Luciano and his operatives were regarded by the two principal protagonists as potential prizes to the victors. However, by twists of cunning and pragmatic collaboration, the coveted prizes became the victors themselves.

While driven by their own purposes, Joe the Boss Masseria and Salvatore Maranzano were, to some extent, dangling on the strings of master puppeteers. In 1931, Luciano was 34 years old, Meyer Lansky 29 — they were young men wanting ostensibly to be left alone to carry on business. In reality, they wanted all of the business. That they got. The Castellammarese War might more aptly be called Luciano's War.

Luciano, Lansky, their partners, and their mentors — Arnold Rothstein in the early years and Johnny Torrio later — were the architects of a criminal enterprise that lasted 50 years before it began to crack. New laws and new technology helped along the process. So did ambitious prosecutors, many using the battle against the Mob to further their own political ambitions. In present times, former mayor of New York City Rudy Giuliani has, perhaps, been the most successful at both.

Epilogue

The Mob may now appear to have fallen on hard times, but its outlaw myths, like the Night of the Vespers, continue to fuel America's fascination with action, adventure, and the pursuit of happiness in a frontier context. As for the hard times, the recent fate of such gangsters as John Gotti, his son, and many others may in part have resulted from their belief in their own propaganda. John Gotti died in prison and his son is doing time — both ratted out by their own soldiers.

Yet, as the outfit has steadily diminished in power, other organized crime groups have risen to take its place. Russian, Chinese, Vietnamese, and Japanese gangs have moved into positions of increased power. They have also found new ways to make money. Drug trafficking has replaced bootlegging as the mother lode of criminal revenue. Fraud, notably credit card and stock fraud, has replaced gambling. Yet some of the money-laundering techniques first implemented by Meyer Lansky are now universally practiced.

Sam Bronfman, a Canadian who built a multimillion-dollar empire selling whiskey to thirsty Americans, usually through buyers such as Luciano, Capone, Dalitz, Johnson, Dwyer, and others, came from impoverished beginnings. He had a theory of cyclical evolution within families: the first generation works in shirt sleeves to build the wealth, the second generation wears silk suits and dissipates the wealth, and the third generation returns to shirtsleeves. Right now, the outfit is nearly back in shirtsleeves.

Further Reading

Balsamo, William and George Carpozi Jr. *Under the Clock: The Inside Story of the Mafia's First 100 Years.* Far Hills, New Jersey: New Horizon Press, 1988.

Eisenberg, Dennis, Uri Dan, and Eli Landau. *Meyer Lansky: Mogul of the Mob.* New York: Paddington Press Ltd., 1979.

Gosch, Martin A. and Richard Hammer. *The Last Testament of Lucky Luciano.* Boston: Little, Brown & Company, 1975.

Lacey, Robert. *Little Man: Meyer Lansky and the Gangster Life.* Boston: Little, Brown & Company, 1991.

NOTE: Particular credit is due to the late Martin Gosch and Richard Hammer for many of the direct quotes attributed to Lucky Luciano.

Author Bio

Ottawa-based Art Montague writes fiction as well as non-fiction, but his interests in history, biography, and crime remain constant. He is a member of Crime Writers of Canada and the Periodical Writers Association of Canada.

AMAZING STORIES
NOW AVAILABLE!

TRUE AMERICAN AMAZING STORIES™

LUCKY LUCIANO

The Father of Organized Crime

GANGSTER
by Cat Klerks

ISBN 1-55265-102-9

AMAZING STORIES
NOW AVAILABLE!

TRUE AMERICAN AMAZING STORIES™

MEYER LANSKY

The Shadowy Exploits of New York's Master Manipulator

GANGSTER
by Art Montague

ISBN 1-55265-100-2

AMAZING STORIES
NOW AVAILABLE!

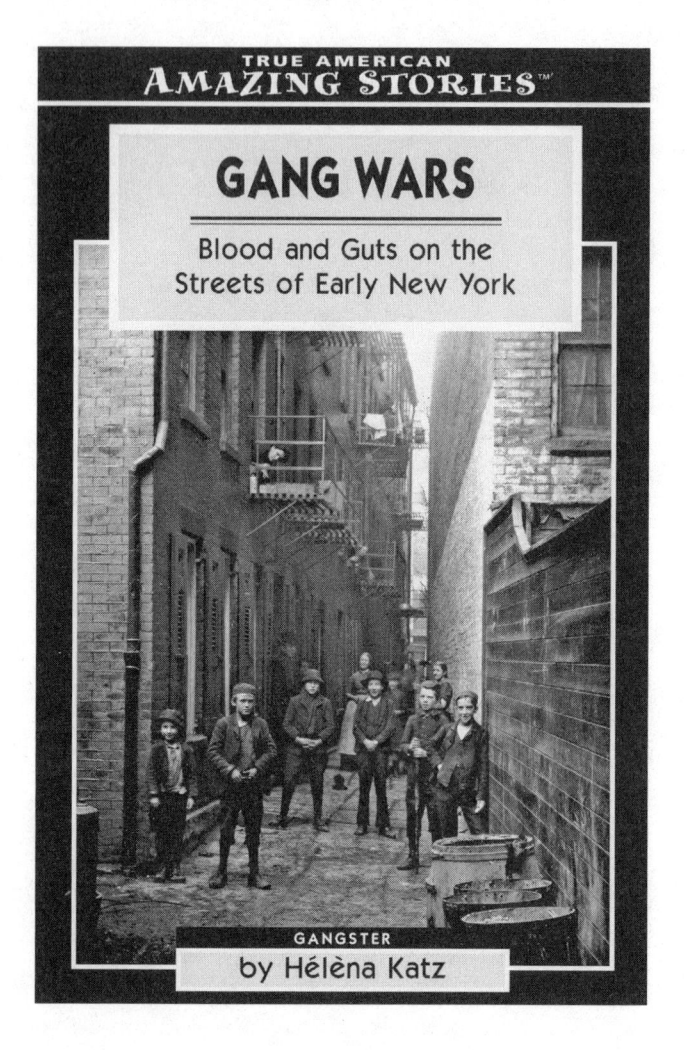

TRUE AMERICAN AMAZING STORIES™

GANG WARS

Blood and Guts on the Streets of Early New York

GANGSTER
by Hélèna Katz

ISBN 1-55265-105-3

AMAZING STORIES

NOW AVAILABLE!

AMAZING STORIES™

LEGENDS, LIARS, AND LAWBREAKERS

Incredible Tales from the Pacific Northwest

HISTORY/CRIME
by Valerie Green

ISBN 1-55153-771-0

AMAZING STORIES
NOW AVAILABLE!

TRUE AMERICAN AMAZING STORIES™

DUTCH SCHULTZ
The Brazen Beer Baron of New York

GANGSTER
by Nate Hendley

ISBN 1-55265-101-0